THE BOOK
OF REVELATION

A BRIEF EXEGETICAL ANALYSIS OF
BIBLE PROPHECY

by

Ioan Logos

aSys Publishing

ISBN: 978-1-910757-77-2

aSys Publishing 2017

http://www.asys-publishing.co.uk

Contents

Preface

The Book of Revelation, or the Apocalypse of John, is the last book of the Bible. It consists of prophetic revelations and visions presented in allegorical language regarding the future events and the end of the world. These visions have been revealed to John who at that time was exiled to a Greek island called Patmos as a result of anti-Christian persecution.

For some believers, the Book of Revelation is a mystery – it is something beyond human comprehension. For others, it is a nourishing ground for promoting speculative and tendentious ideologies. However, for sincere and devout believers, it is a message of hope and encouragement urging them to remain faithful until the end.

Differences of opinion regarding prophetic interpretation of the beasts of Revelation often bring about confusion among believers. This book sheds new light on the understanding of these prophetic allegories and at the same time combats erroneous and tendentious interpretations.

The material of this book derives from my previous publication, Adventist Prophetic Fable. It came as a separate book out of necessity for those who are particularly interested in the Book of Revelation. A brief introductory and conclusive material was elaborated to substantiate the message of this work and emphasize its particularity – prophetic and apocalyptic value within believer's life.

Acknowledgement

This book is dedicated to the One, prophetically described as
who is, who was, and who is to come
– the Lord Jesus Christ –

trusting that its public appearance will meet His divine
blessing, and that its message will reach sincere hearts of those
who long to know the truth.

The beast with seven heads and ten horns

"¹ and [a]he stood upon the sand of the sea. And I saw a beast coming up out of the sea, having ten horns and seven heads, and on his horns ten diadems, and upon his heads names of blasphemy.

² And the beast which I saw was like unto a leopard, and his feet were as the feet of a bear, and his mouth as the mouth of a lion: and the dragon gave him his power, and his throne, and great authority.

³ And I saw one of his heads as though it had been [b]smitten unto death; and his death-stroke was healed: and the whole earth wondered after the beast" (Rev. 13:1-3).

"³ And he carried me away in the Spirit into a wilderness: and I saw a woman sitting upon a scarlet-colored beast, [a]full of names of blasphemy, having seven heads and ten horns" (Rev. 17:3).

"⁶ And I saw the woman drunken with the blood of the saints, and with the blood of the [e]martyrs of Jesus. And when I saw her, I wondered with a great wonder" (Rev. 17:6).

"⁸ The beast that thou sawest was, and is not; and is about to come up out of the abyss, [f]and to go into perdition. And they that dwell on the earth shall wonder, they whose name hath not been written [g] in the book of life from the foundation of the world, when they behold the beast, how that he was, and is not, and [h]shall come" (Rev. 17:8).

1

"9 Here is the [i]mind that hath wisdom. The seven heads are seven mountains, on which the woman sitteth: 10 and [j]they are seven kings; the five are fallen, the one is, the other is not yet come; and when he cometh, he must continue a little while. 11 And the beast that was, and is not, is himself also an eighth, and is of the seven; and he goeth into perdition" (Rev. 17:9-11).

The Book of Revelation plays a central role in Christian eschatology. Its prophetic message has always been the subject of intense debate and speculation, as it deals with sensitive topics concerning the end of the world and the Second Coming of Jesus Christ.

The book starts with a blessing and ends with a warning:

"3 Blessed is he that readeth, and they that hear the words of the prophecy, and keep the things that are written therein: for the time is at hand" (Rev. 1:3).

"18 I testify unto every man that heareth the words of the prophecy of this book, If any man shall add [s]unto them, God shall add [t]unto him the plagues which are written in this book: 19 and if any man shall take away from the words of the book of this prophecy, God shall take away his part from the tree of life, and out of the holy city, [u]which are written in this book" (Rev. 22:18-19).

Apocalyptic message of the book is astonishing. For many centuries, believers have devoted much time and effort to studying and solving prophetic allegories of the Book of Revelation. Sincere believers felt blessed for what they read and understood; however, those whose real intent was to give the prophecy a particular course resorted to tendentious interpretations. There are many speculations over the identity of the beasts of Revelation, and many attempts have been made to give it a reasonable explanation; however, some of those interpretations prove to be simply a product of the human imagination. According to the Bible, false prophecies have pernicious consequences on believers who accept them. From a historical perspective, there is strong evidence confirming the fact that erroneous or tendentious interpretation of Bible prophecy has a powerful effect on people – that of instigating religious conflicts which often lead to the loss of human lives.

The Book of Revelation has puzzled Christians for many centuries. For some believers, each major historical event became a source of inspiration for new interpretations of Bible prophecy. The Book of Revelation goes hand in hand with the Book of Daniel – the two books to a considerable extent compensate each other prophetically. Therefore, to understand prophetic meaning of these mysterious apocalyptic prophecies, simultaneous study of both books is absolutely indispensable.

Some Bible scholars assert that historic event of 476, when the last western Roman emperor, Romulus Augustulus, was deposed by Germanic peoples lead by Odoacer and the Western Roman Empire collapsed (a fatal wound to the Roman Empire), is the fulfillment of prophecy "*I saw one of his heads as though it had been [b]smitten unto death . . .*" described in Revelation 13:3. They assert that the "*ten horns*" (Rev. 13:1; Dan. 7:24) are ten European nations, which arose after the fall of Rome and the Western Roman Empire, that the "*little horn*" before whom three of the first horns were plucked up by the root (Dan. 7:8) represents the Papacy, and that the "*three horns plucked up by the root*" represent three Arian peoples (Heruli, Vandals, and Ostrogoths), which were eradicated by Rome (with significant help of the Byzantine army). This version is vehemently supported by Seventh-day Adventist Church.

According to these scholars, the allegory "*and his*

death-stroke was healed..." (Rev. 13:3) represents the revived Western Roman Empire, later known as the Holy Roman Empire. At first impression, this reasoning seems to be quite plausible; however, two vital facts are being neglected:

1) The beast looked like a "*leopard, bear, and lion*" (Rev. 13:2).

2) The prophecy clearly identified the Roman Empire as the "*one is*", not as the "*five are fallen*" (Rev. 17:10). Therefore, the so-called revived Western Roman Empire cannot be the head whose "*death-stroke was healed*", that is, the beast described as "*was, and is not, is himself also an eighth, and is of the seven*" (Rev. 17:11).

Supporters of this prophetic interpretation have been indoctrinated with the teaching that historic event of 1798, when Pope Pius VI was arrested by Berthier (one of Napoleon's generals) and imprisoned in citadel of Valence in France where he later died, marked the fulfillment of "*42 months (1260 days) or 1260 years*" prophecy of Revelation 13:5. Therefore, historic event of 1798 marked the end of 1260 years of Papal supremacy (538-1798) – a fatal wound inflicted on Papacy. Such religious conviction, however, proves to be faulty as follows:

1) According to this interpretation, there seem to be two deadly wounds (one in 476, another in 1798).

2) Revelation 13:3 states very clearly that "*one of his heads*" (that is, one of the seven heads) seemed to have been fatally wounded – it does not say "*one of his horns*", that is, one of the ten horns, as the beast had seven heads and ten horns (Rev. 13:1). Linguistically, head and horn represent two different words with different meanings; anatomically, these have a totally different structure and function. Should head and horn, prophetically, be considered identical?

It is quite evident that such interpretation of Bible prophecy is questionable. Therefore, after a thorough analysis of this issue, inevitable remarks follow:

- The "*ten horns*" represent ten kings (kingdoms) that ascended after the fall of the Roman Empire, prophetically identified as "*legs of iron*" (Dan. 2:33, 40); the ten horns also seem to be "*ten toes*" of the prophetic statue of the Book of Daniel (Dan. 2:28-45). Feet and toes "*part of iron, and part of clay*" represent a new empire that succeeded the Roman Empire. Feet and toes "*partly of iron*" represent former Roman territories within that new empire;

- Prophetic allegory "*ten horns*" described in the Book of Daniel and the Book of Revelation seems to give an impression of discordance. The ten horns of Daniel 7:7 seem to be related to the fourth empire (Roman Empire); however, Daniel 7:24 provide an additional detail: "*ten horns*" arise after the fall of the fourth empire. The Roman Empire was ruled by many Caesars, not by ten kings (ten horns). In the Book of Revelation, the "*ten horns*" do not appear to be part of the Roman Empire. In Revelation, these horns constitute a new empire, as they receive power as kings one hour with the beast (Rev. 17:12), which is described as "*was, and is not; and is about to come up*", and which is also described as looking like a "*leopard, bear, and lion*" having "*ten crowns*" on its horns (Rev. 13:1). If "*ten horns*" also represent "*ten toes*", then the version according to which "*ten horns*" represent ten European nations that arose after the fall of the Western Roman Empire is contradictory, as the two iron legs of the Roman Empire continued with feet and five toes on each foot – the expression "Western Roman leg with a foot having ten toes", thus Eastern Roman leg with a foot without toes, is irrational. However, as, according to the Book of Revelation, the beast looked like a "*leopard, bear, and lion*", and as it "*was, and is not; and is about to come up*", it is pertinent to say that the "*ten horns*" are predominantly related to the Middle East and to what once was the Byzantine Empire (Eastern Roman leg). Therefore, ten horns or kings (kingdoms) arose after the fall of the Roman Empire, and definitive fall of the Roman Empire took place in 1453, the date when Constantinople – Christian bastion of the Eastern Roman Empire – was conquered by the Ottoman Turks. The Western Roman Empire (western iron leg) fell almost one thousand years earlier, in 476;

- It is pertinent to suggest that the "*little horn*" (Dan. 7:8, 24), which uprooted three other horns, and which is different from the earlier ones, represents the rise of Islamic Empire, and that "*three plucked up by the rooted horns*" must be three horns of the divided Greek Empire (kingdoms of Seleucus, Ptolemy, and Lysimachus), which, to some extent, were also part of the Eastern Roman Empire later being absorbed into the Islam Empire. The rise of Muslim Empire, which allegorically in Revelation chapter 9 seems to be described as "*locusts*" coming out of the smoke, which arose from the "*pit of the abyss*", was allowed to make war on Christians and Jews and defeat them;

- Regarding the verse "*I considered the horns, and behold, there came up among them <u>another horn, a little one</u>, before which three of the first horns were plucked up by the roots . . .* " (Dan. 7:8), the following explanation is suggested: the "*little horn*", by uprooting three of the first horns (kings), takes possession of three kingdoms and revives one of the seven heads prophetically described as "*was, and is not, is himself also an eighth, and is of the seven*" (Rev. 17:11);

- Prophetic allegory "*feet part of iron, and part of clay*" (Dan. 2:33, 40-42) is self-explanatory: iron represents the Roman Empire; clay suggests something else, from outside, not Roman. Therefore, this refers to a new empire, which consisted partly of conquered territory once belonging to the Roman Empire and partly of territory that was beyond the Roman border (new conquests in the Middle East, Central Asia, and Africa).

Some believers assert that prophetic beast with seven heads and ten horns described in the Book of Revelation chapters 13 and 17 is not the same beast. That is not quite so. These two chapters compensate each other, thus offer a more detailed picture of this mysterious beast. Revelation chapter 13 informs the reader that the beast "*coming up out of the sea*" comes up from among the peoples, kingdoms prophetically described as "*leopard, bear, and lion*" – the incipient phase of that empire. The (scarlet) beast of Revelation chapter 17 described as "*about to come up out of the abyss*" represents the final phase of that empire – a time following the prophetic event described as "*...I saw a star from heaven fallen unto the earth: and there was given to him the key of the pit of the abyss*" (Rev. 9:1), a time when the "*harlot (great city)*" becomes so spiritually depraved that she must be punished.

The central issue in Revelation chapters 13 and 17 is less the beast (empire) as such, but rather the destructive satanic power exercised through such earthly authority. However, it is essential to know the true identity of this apocalyptic beast.

The beast with seven heads and ten horns presents certain particularities:

- The red dragon having "*seven heads and ten horns, and upon his heads seven diadems*" (Rev. 12:3) represents satanic power exercised through earthly empires during the reign of the "*seven heads*", probably before Satan was cast out of heaven;

- The beast having "*ten horns and seven heads, and on his horns ten diadems*" (Rev. 13:1) represents satanic power exercised during the reign of the "*ten horns*", that is, through ten kings (kingdoms) that ruled within the new empire that arose after the fall of the Roman Empire, probably after Satan was cast out of heaven to earth (Rev. 12:7-9);

- The verse "*And he carried me away in the Spirit into a wilderness: and I saw a woman sitting upon a scarlet-colored beast,* [a]*full of names of blasphemy, having seven heads and ten horns*" (Rev. 17:3) is an extension of the prophetic picture described in Revelation 13:1. However, Revelation chapter 17 is focusing exclusively on the head (beast) whose wound is <u>healed</u>. Here, an extra element is added: the "*woman.*"

According to Revelation 13:1-2, if our Bible is a reliable translation of the original manuscripts, the beast was like "<u>*unto a leopard*</u>", and his feet were as the "*feet of <u>a bear</u>*", and his mouth as the "*mouth of <u>a lion</u>.*" This means that the beast looked like Greek, Medo-Persian, and Babylonian Empires (Dan. 2:31-45; 7:1-17) – the Roman Empire is missing. On the other hand, the beast, according to Revelation chapter 17, ascends from the bottomless pit in the wilderness (desert) and is presented as "<u>*was, and is not, is himself also an eighth, and is of the seven*</u>" (Rev. 17:3, 8, 11) – when John received the Revelation, the Roman Empire was not one of the "*five fallen heads (empires)*", in fact, the Roman Empire is prophetically described as "*one is*" (Rev. 17:10). In both cases, the Roman Empire has no relevance to this prophetic beast. In other words, the beast is related to the Middle East, to the wilderness (desert). This is a clear description of the new empire that ascends after the fall of the Roman Empire – the rise of Muslim Empire.

Once again, the beast (the "*eighth king*"), which "<u>*was, and is not; and is about to come up*</u> *out of the abyss*", is one of the seven, that is, one of the "<u>*five fallen heads*</u> *(empires).*" John received the Revelation in the late first century. At this time, the Roman Empire was a prosperous empire thus could not be one of the "*five fallen heads (empires)*" – the Roman Empire identifies with the "*sixth head*" prophetically described as the "*one is.*" Furthermore, the Roman Empire has never been prophetically described as "*ascending out of the earth*", that is to say, "*coming up out of the abyss.*"

Let's compare the following verses:

> *"And I saw one of his heads as though it had been*

[b]smitten unto death; and his death-stroke was healed…" (Rev. 13:3);

"The beast that thou sawest was, and is not; and is about to come up out of the abyss, [f]and to go into perdition…" (Rev. 17:8);

"And the beast that was, and is not, is himself also an eighth, and is of the seven; and he goeth into perdition" (Rev. 17:11);

Let's draw another parallelism:

3) a. *"one of his heads as though it had been [b]smitten unto death"* (Rev. 13:3);
   b. *"the beast that thou sawest was"* (Rev. 17:8);
   c. *"five are fallen"* (Rev. 17:10).

4) *"is not"* (Rev. 17:8), that is, the beast *"is not"* when John received the Revelation.

5) a. *"his death-stroke was healed"* (Rev. 13:3);
   b. *"is about to come out of the abyss"* (Rev. 17:8);
   c. *"the beast that was, and is not, is himself also an eighth, and is of the seven…"* (Rev. 17:11).

It is pertinent to assert that all quotations mentioned above (*"smitten unto death"* head, his *"death-stroke was healed"*, the beast *"that was, and is not"*) identify one and the same head: the *"eighth king"*, which *"is of the seven."*

The following verses also confirm the identity of one and the same beast:

"8 And all that dwell on the earth shall [h]worship him, <u>every one whose name hath not been [i]written from the foundation of the world in the book of life</u> of the Lamb that hath been slain" (Rev. 13:8).

"⁸...And they that dwell on the earth shall wonder, they whose name hath not been written [g]in the book of life from the foundation of the world, when they behold the beast, how that he was, and is not, and [h]shall come" (Rev. 17:8).

According to the New Testament, it would be nonsense to say that the verse *"they whose names hath not been written in the book of life of the Lamb"* (Rev. 13:8; Rev. 17:8) refers to Christians – believers who accepted the *"word of God, and the testimony of Jesus."* On the contrary, it is common sense to affirm that those *"whose names are not written in the book of life of the Lamb"* are the ones who do not accept *"Jesus Christ and His testimony"* – these must be the "non-Christians."

Once again, from the perspective of the New Testament, it is unbiblical to say that prophetic expression *"they whose names are not written in the book of life..."* (Rev. 13:8; Rev. 17:8), which refers to those who worship the beast that looks like a *"leopard, bear, and lion"* (Rev. 13:1-2), and that *"was, and is not; and is about to come up out of the abyss"* (Rev. 17:3, 7), applies to Christian believers. On the contrary, these verses refer to those who are not Christians. In support of this statement, it is appropriate to quote Jesus' prayer on the night of His arrest:

"⁶ I manifested thy name unto the men whom thou gavest me out of the world: thine they were, and thou gavest them to me; and they have kept thy word. ⁷ Now they know that all things whatsoever thou hast given me are from thee: ⁸ for the words which thou gavest me I have given unto them; and they received them, and knew of a truth that I came forth from thee, and they believed that thou didst send me. ⁹ I [b]pray for them: I [c]pray not for the world, but for those whom thou hast given me;

*for they are thine: [10] and all things that are mine
are thine, and thine are mine: and I am glorified in
them" (Jn. 17:6-10).*

Prophetic allegory *"seven heads and ten horns"* as such is
a mystery. However, Revelation chapter 17 provides details
regarding the identity of the *"seven heads"* and *"ten horns"* as
follows:

*"[9] Here is the [i]mind that hath wisdom. The seven
heads are seven mountains, on which the woman
sitteth: [10] and [j]they are seven kings; the five are
fallen, the one is, the other is not yet come; and
when he cometh, he must continue a little while.
[11] And the beast that was, and is not, is himself also
an eighth, and is of the seven; and he goeth into
perdition" (Rev. 17:9-11).*

*"[12] And the ten horns that thou sawest are ten
kings, who have received no kingdom as yet; but
they receive authority as kings, with the beast, for
one hour" (Rev. 17:12).*

*"[15] And he saith unto me, The waters which thou
sawest, where the harlot sitteth, are peoples, and
multitudes, and nations, and tongues" (Rev. 17:15).*

The beasts described in Revelation 13:1-3 and 17:3, 7-8 have in
common the following characteristics:

1) Both beasts have *"seven heads and ten horns."*

2) Both beasts exclude the Roman Empire. The following
   verses confirm it:

   *"[2] And the beast which I saw was like unto a
   leopard, and his feet were as the feet of a bear, and
   his mouth as the mouth of a lion: and the dragon*

11

gave him his power, and his throne, and great authority" (Rev. 13:2).

"⁹ Here is the [i]mind that hath wisdom. _The seven heads are seven mountains_, on which the woman sitteth: ¹⁰ and [j]_they are seven kings; the five are fallen, the one is_, the other is not yet come; and when he cometh, he must continue a little while. ¹¹ And _the beast that was, and is not, is himself also an eighth, and is of the seven_; and he goeth into perdition" (Rev. 17:9-11).

"¹² And _the ten horns that thou sawest are ten kings, who have received no kingdom as yet_; but they receive authority as kings, with the beast, for one hour" (Rev. 17:12).

3) Both beasts exercise their power during the reign of the "_ten horns._" The following verses confirm it:

"¹ and [a]_he stood upon the sand of the sea. And I saw a beast coming up out of the sea, having ten horns and seven heads, and on his horns ten diadems_, and upon his heads names of blasphemy" (Rev. 13:1).

"¹² And _the ten horns that thou sawest are ten kings_, who have received no kingdom as yet; but _they receive authority as kings, with the beast, for one hour_. ¹³ These have one mind, and they give their power and authority unto the be" (Rev. 17:12-13).

4) There is a clear similarity in the following prophetic description: a) "And I saw _one of his heads_ as though it had been [b]_smitten unto death_", and "_his death-stroke was healed_" (Rev. 13:3); b) "_was, and is not; and is about to come up_ out of the abyss…" (Rev. 17:8), and "_was, and_

12

is not, is himself also an eighth, and is of the seven" (Rev. 17:11). Both descriptions identify one and the same head. In other words, one of the heads (empires), which in the first century was no more (when John received the Revelation), will rise again.

5) Prophetic characteristic in the verses below must be attributed to one and the same beast:

> "*8 And all that dwell on the earth shall [h]worship him, every one whose name hath not been [i]written from the foundation of the world in the book of life of the Lamb that hath been slain*" (Rev. 13:8).

> "*8 …And they that dwell on the earth shall wonder, they whose name hath not been written [g]in the book of life from the foundation of the world, when they behold the beast, how that he was, and is not, and [h]shall come*" (Rev. 17:8).

The central issue in Revelation chapter 13 regarding the beast with "*seven heads and ten horns*" is the deadly wounded head, whose "*deadly wound was healed*" (Rev. 13:3), not the seven heads. The central issue in Revelation chapter 17 is also the head (or king) identified as the beast that "*was, and is not, is himself also an eighth, and is of the seven*" (Rev. 17:11). Therefore, both chapters (13 and 17) concentrate on one head, not seven heads – one head with ten horns (Rev. 17:11-12). According to Revelation chapter 17, seven heads represent a succession of kings, kingdom – each head had dominion at a particular time in human history.

Revelation chapters 13 and 17 describes one and the beast (empire) – the two chapters compensate each other. Revelation chapter 13 is focusing on the beast at its incipient phase, while Revelation chapter 17 describes the beast at final phase of its existence. Once again, the two chapters describe one and the same beast. Mystery and complexity of prophetic events described in the Book of Revelation is astonishing – the Holy Spirit speaks to the believers in allegorical language.

Such an approach of Bible prophecy may be regarded as inconsistent because a very important fact is missing: the "*woman (great city, Babylon the Great), which sits on seven mountains, on many waters.*" Certain believers have been indoctrinated with the teaching that the "*woman dressed in purple and scarlet*" sitting on the beast represents Rome and the Roman Catholic Church. Their logic is based on the fact that Rome was built on seven hills. These hills[1] are: *Aventinus, Caelius, Capitolinus, Esquilinus, Palatinus, Quirinalis, Viminalis*. It seems that, deliberately or out of ignorance, they neglect geographical and historical fact that *Collis (Mons) Vaticanus*[1], the hill on which Vatican city was built, is not counted among the traditional seven hills of Rome – Vatican is located across the river Tiber.

Rome has been playing a pivotal role historically, politically, and religiously for many centuries, and for a certain period of time ruled over many kings and nations. Whether or not Rome represents prophetic allegory "*woman sitting upon the beast*", one fact should not be neglected: Rome is not the only great city built on seven hills. Constantinople and Jerusalem were also built on seven hills. Some venture to say that Mecca is surrounded by seven hills (mountains). However, the Book of Revelation clearly states that the woman sits on "*seven mountains*", not on seven hills. Accurate translation of the original Greek manuscript contains the words "*seven mountains*"; yet translators of certain Bible versions permitted themselves the arrogance to replace "*seven mountains*" with seven hills.

Constantinople (New Rome), the capital of the Eastern Roman (Byzantine) Empire until 1453, was also built on seven hills[2]. The city was renamed Istanbul and became the capital of the Ottoman Empire. This city was of vital importance in both empires; however, it lacks prophetic image of the "*woman (whore)*" described in the Book of Revelation.

Jerusalem was also built on seven hills[3][4]. These are[3]: *Mount Gared, Mount Goath, Mount Acra, Mount Bezetha, Mount Moriah, Mount Ophel, and Mount Zion*. For whatever reason, Mt. Gared, Mt. Goath, Mt. Acra, and Mt. Bezetha have been deleted from nearly all maps of Jerusalem; other scholars replaced these with four other mountains: Mount of Olives, Mount of Offence, Mount of Evil Counsel, and Mount Calvary. Nowadays, many cities have the reputation of being built on seven hills[4]. Most of them, however, have no relevance to the Bible prophecy.

The "*seven heads*" on which the woman sits represent "*seven kings (kingdoms)*." But this is a succession of kings (kingdoms), as the Bible gives us a clue: "*the five are fallen, the one is, the other is not yet come*", that is to say, a fallen king (kingdom) is succeeded by another one ... and so on. John's apocalyptic visions represent a description of the events to come – visions of the future. All these prophetic heads (kings, kingdoms) have one thing in common: the "*woman (great harlot)*" with whom the kings of the earth have committed fornication and the inhabitants of the earth have been made drunk with the wine of her fornication (Rev. 17:1-3, 18). This apocalyptic woman is described as:

> "*5 and upon her forehead a name written, [d]Mystery, Babylon the Great, the Mother of the Harlots and of the Abominations of the Earth*" (Rev. 17:5).

> "*6 And I saw the woman drunken with the blood of the saints, and with the blood of the [e]martyrs of Jesus. And when I saw her, I wondered with a great wonder*" (Rev. 17:6).

Several cities have the reputation of being involved in persecuting and killing God's people – all those who keep God's commandments, and have the testimony of Jesus Christ. These are: Jerusalem, Rome, and Istanbul. According to the Bible, Jerusalem is the place where initial persecution of Christians began. Pagan Rome persecuted Christians for several centuries; Christian Rome persecuted those believers whose religious views were considered by the church as heretical. Istanbul, the capital of the Ottoman Islamic Empire, is the place where for several centuries were conceived military strategies to invade and conquer Christian territories, the city where were issued orders that resulted in direct and systematic persecution and atrocities against Christians and Jews. On the other hand, one should not neglect Mecca – the holiest city in Islam [home of the greatest Islamic mosque surrounding the Kaaba[5] (a cuboid building with the "Black Stone" on its eastern corner), the holiest Islamic site], the birthplace of Muhammad, the heart of Islam (Muslims face the direction of Mecca when they pray, they face Kaaba)[5]. Islam began in Mecca. Muslim military expansion that established a huge Muslim Empire bringing along religious persecution and atrocities against those who rejected Islamic religion also commenced in Mecca. Thus, all these cities represent probable candidates for the title "*Babylon the Great, the Mother of Harlots and Abominations of the Earth.*"

Again, some believers assert that prophetic allegory the "*woman sitting upon a scarlet-coloured beast*" represents Rome. Such allegation, however, is marked by inconsistency. As mentioned previously, the beast with seven heads and ten horns is described as:

> "…*was like unto a <u>leopard</u>, and his feet were as the feet of a <u>bear</u>, and his mouth as the mouth of a <u>lion</u>…" (Rev. 13:2).*

> "…*<u>was, and is not; and is about to come up</u> out of the abyss…" (Rev. 17:8).*

> "…*<u>was, and is not</u>, is himself also an eighth, <u>and is</u>*

16

Such prophetic description cannot be attributed to the Roman Empire in any form; therefore, prophetic allegory the *"woman (harlot)"* sitting upon the beast, which does not represent the Roman Empire, cannot be attributed to Rome.

The topic "Rome fell in 476 AD", that is, the Roman Empire received a "fatal wound in 476" is questionable. It is a fact that Rome had been sacked several times (in 410, 455...), but not in 476. Historic event of 476 refers to the deposition of the last western Roman emperor, Romulus Aurelius, who resided in Ravenna, the new capital of the Western Roman Empire at that time. Thus, year 476 marks the fall the Western Roman Empire and the end of the imperial glory of Rome. However, in 324, Emperor Constantine transferred the imperial capital from Rome to Constantinople – the New Rome. Eastern Roman Empire with its capital at Constantinople continued its dominion for almost another thousand years. Emperors of the Eastern Roman Empire (Byzantine Empire) undertook several attempts to restore the Western Roman Empire, that is, to bring back the Roman Empire to its original glory. By 1453, the date when Constantinople was conquered by the Muslim Turks, Rome has considerably recovered from its 5th century decline and fall; however, this is a different Rome – a Christian Rome. Western Europe, under the influence of Rome, fought many battles against Muslims. This includes the famous battles like: the battle of Tours (732) against the Saracens, the battle of Lepanto (1571) against the Ottoman fleet, and the battle of Vienna (1683) against the Ottomans – the three battles stopped Islamic invasion of Western Christianity. In other words, the topic regarding the fall of the Roman Empire is questionable. However, it is reasonable to assert that complete collapse of the Roman Empire took place in 1453, not in 476.

Once again, believers with radical views may argue vehemently that prophetic allegory the *"woman sitting upon a* scarlet-coloured beast, [a]full of names of blasphemy, having seven heads and ten horns" refers to Rome, as this city was involved in religious persecution of Jews, Christians, Muslims, and so on. Rome's variable role throughout its history is quite well known. As it was mentioned previously, the following apocalyptic verses do not identify the Western Roman Empire or Rome:

> "2 And _the beast which I saw was like unto a leopard_, and his feet were as the feet of _a bear_, and his mouth as the mouth of _a lion_: and the dragon gave him his power, and his throne, and great authority" (Rev. 13:2).

> "8 _The beast that thou sawest was, and is not; and is about to come up out of the abyss,_ [f]_and to go into perdition. And they that dwell on the earth shall wonder, they whose name hath not been written [g] in the book of life from the foundation of the world, when they behold the beast, how that he was, and is not, and [h]shall come_" (Rev. 17:8).

> "9 Here is the [i]mind that hath wisdom. _The seven heads are seven mountains, on which the woman sitteth_: 10 and [j]_they are seven kings; the five are fallen, the one is_, the other is not yet come; and when he cometh, he must continue a little while. 11 And _the beast that was, and is not, is himself also an eighth, and is of the seven_; and he goeth into perdition" (Rev. 17:9-11).

> "12 And _the ten horns_ that thou sawest _are ten kings_, who have received no kingdom as yet; but _they receive authority as kings, with the beast, for one hour_" (Rev. 17:12).

The beast with seven heads and ten horns, which "_was, and_

is not" (when John received the Apocalypse), and which is also "*an eighth, and is of the seven*", that is to say, one of the "*five are fallen*", cannot be the Roman Empire. Therefore, this excludes the possibility that Rome prophetically represents the "*woman (harlot)*" sitting upon a scarlet-coloured beast (Rev. 17:3). Furthermore, Rome is not the only city built on seven hills.

Christian Rome was involved in military campaigns against Muslims. On the other hand, military interventions and judicial institutions were used to combat the spread of teachings considered by the church as heretical. It is a fact that military actions often result in the loss of human lives, which is not in harmony with Christ's two commandments of love (Mt. 22:36-40). Nevertheless, an unbiased analyst will not leave unnoticed the fact that, despite certain controversial doctrines and certain mistakes committed in the past, Rome (the Catholic Church) has been playing for many centuries a pivotal role in defending Christianity from Muslim religious militaristic ambitions, and from pseudo-Christian teachings polluting the Western Christianity. There is no doubt that, to some extent, such fundamental ecclesiastical task was susceptible to human errors. Acute religious crisis within Christianity was felt especially after the Ottoman conquest of Constantinople – the bastion and ecclesiastical centre of the Orthodox Christianity. For many Christians, Rome – the ecclesiastical centre of the Catholic Christianity – was the only hope and consolation during the centuries-long Muslim threats to the Western Christianity. On the other hand, it is pertinent to mention that alliances (official or secretive) with the Ottoman Empire were sometimes convenient for certain European leaders and influential individuals.

As mentioned earlier, certain believers will object to such prophetic interpretation. By quoting Daniel 7:7, these believers will insist that "*ten horns*" are related to the Roman Empire. At this point, it seems that Daniel 7:7 is in prophetic discordance with Revelation 17:10-12, 16. Adherents of this version, however, ought to give veritable explanation to the following remarks:

1) The beast with seven heads and ten horns looks like a "*leopard, bear, and lion*" (Rev. 13:1-2) – geographically, such description corresponds to the Middle East territory (Islamic countries); therefore, the "*ten horns*" also ought to identify with "*leopard, bear, and lion.*"

2) The beast "<u>*that was, and is not*</u> *(the eighth king)*" is one of the seven heads (empires), that is, one of the "<u>*five fallen heads.*</u>" The Roman Empire, when John received the Revelation, was a prosperous empire – prophetically, Roman Empire is the "*sixth head*", not one of the "*five are fallen*" (Rev. 17:9-10). The "<u>*ten horns*</u>" receive power as kings for an hour with the beast described as "*was, and is not, and is about to come up*" (Rev. 17:12) – this beast cannot identify with the Roman Empire.

3) The alleged ten horns rising after the fall of the Western Roman Empire make war against the Lamb of God (Rev. 17:14).

4) The ten horns (allegedly ten Western European Christian nations) and the beast (allegedly the revived Western Roman Empire, the Holy Roman Empire) hate the whore (allegedly Rome, the Catholic Church), make her desolate and destroy her with fire (Rev. 17:16) – self-destruction.

5) Why would Christians destroy each other? Why would they destroy Vatican (Rome) – the heart of over a billion Catholic Christians?

6) The prophecy states very clearly: the seven heads are "*seven mountains*", not seven hills (Rev. 17:9). The seven mountains are also seven kings/kingdoms (Rev. 17:10). The

"*woman*" sits upon many waters, and these are peoples, multitudes, nations, and languages (Rev. 17:1, 15). The "*woman*" is the great city that rules over the kings of the earth (Rev. 17:18).

Nowadays, Rome stands firm and logically there isn't any potential threat of destruction of Rome by the European nations, which arose after the fall of the Western Roman Empire. The problem with prophetic interpretation based on the prophecy of Daniel chapter 7 concerning the identity of the "*ten horns*" is that there are only four empires mentioned – the rise of the new empire (Islamic Empire), which conquered a considerable territory of the fourth empire (Roman Empire), is missing. It seems that some believers have to choose between Daniel 7:7-8 and Revelation chapter 17. The Book of Revelation, however, should be a priority for believers under the new covenant. It is very evident that this apocalyptic beast represents the Islamic Empire and ten horns represent ten Muslim kings; therefore, it would be unreasonable to assert that Rome rules over Muslim kings. There was no Islam, when Rome was reigning over the kings of the earth – the Islamic Empire rose after the fall of Rome – therefore, there must be another city that identifies this prophetic allegory!

On the other hand, in the Book of Revelation are mentioned prophetic numbers that make reference to the time and duration of prophetic events:

> "*2 And the court which is without the [c]temple [d] leave without, and measure it not; for it hath been given unto the [e]nations: and the holy city shall they tread under foot forty and two months*" (Rev. 11:2).

> "*3 And I will give unto my two witnesses, and they shall prophesy a thousand two hundred and three-score days, clothed in sackcloth*" (Rev. 11:3).

"⁶ And the woman fled into the wilderness, where she hath a place prepared of God, that there they may nourish her <u>a thousand two hundred and threescore days</u>" (Rev. 12:6).

"¹⁴ And there were given to the woman the two wings of the great eagle, that she might fly into the wilderness unto her place, where she is nourished <u>for a time, and times, and half a time</u>, from the face of the serpent" (Rev. 12:14).

"⁵ and there was given to him a mouth speaking great things and blasphemies; and there was given to him authority [e]to continue <u>forty and two months</u>" (Rev. 13:5).

If we apply "day-year" principle (see: Num. 14:34; Ezek. 4:5-6; Dan. 9:24-27), we get the following proportion: 42 months equals 1260 days, and 1260 days equals 1260 years. As to the prophecy concerning the *"holy city being tread under foot"* (Rev. 11:2), there are no historical evidence to confirm that Rome, that is, the Roman Empire (in any form) trampled on the Holy City (Jerusalem) for such a long period of time. However, the history confirms that Jerusalem was occupied and controlled by Muslims for a very long period of time – more then twelve centuries.

The Book of Revelation provides a clue regarding the identity of the *"mystery woman"*:

"⁶ And I saw <u>the woman drunken with the blood of the saints, and with the blood of the [e]martyrs of Jesus</u>. And when I saw her, I wondered with a great wonder" (Rev. 17:6).

"²⁰ <u>Rejoice over her</u>, thou heaven, and ye saints, and <u>ye apostles, and ye prophets</u>; for God hath judged your judgment on her" (Rev. 18:20).

"24 And in her was found the blood of prophets and of saints, and of all that have been slain upon the earth" (Rev. 18:24).

Biblically, one city fits this description; only one city "*killest the prophets*" – that city is Jerusalem. The following Bible verses confirm it:

"37 O Jerusalem, Jerusalem, that killeth the prophets, and stoneth them that are sent unto her! how often would I have gathered thy children together, even as a hen gathereth her chickens under her wings, and ye would not! 38 Behold, your house is left unto you [p]desolate" (Mat. 23:37-38).

"33 Nevertheless I must go on my way to-day and to-morrow and the day following: for it cannot be that a prophet perish out of Jerusalem. 34 O Jerusalem, Jerusalem, that killeth the prophets, and stoneth them that are sent unto her! how often would I have gathered thy children together, even as a hen gathereth her own brood under her wings, and ye would not!" (Lk. 13:33-34).

"47 Woe unto you! for ye build the tombs of the prophets, and your fathers killed them. 48 So ye are witnesses and consent unto the works of your fathers: for they killed them, and ye build their tombs. 49 Therefore also said the wisdom of God, I will send unto them prophets and apostles; and some of them they shall kill and persecute; 50 that the blood of all the prophets, which was shed from the foundation of the world, may be required of this generation; 51 from the blood of Abel unto the blood of Zachariah, who perished between the altar and the [x]sanctuary: yea, I say unto you, it

shall be required of this generation" (Lk. 11:47-51).

"[8] And their [g]dead bodies lie in the street of the great city, which spiritually is called Sodom and Egypt, where also their Lord was crucified" (Rev. 11:8).

Biblical and prophetic role of Jerusalem in God's plan is indisputable – a reality confirmed in both the Old and New Testament. However, according to the Old Testament, Jerusalem was also called "*harlot*" by Yahweh, the God of Israel, as follows:

"The vision of Isaiah the son of Amoz, which he saw concerning Judah and Jerusalem, in the days of Uzziah, Jotham, Ahaz, and Hezekiah, kings of Judah. [2] Hear, heavens, and listen, earth; for Yahweh[a] has spoken: "I have nourished and brought up children, and they have rebelled against me ... [21] How the faithful city has become a prostitute! She was full of justice; righteousness lodged in her, but now murderers" (Is. 1:1-2, 21).

"[1] Again Yahweh's word came to me, saying, [2] Son of man, cause Jerusalem to know her abominations [1]Again the word of the LORD came unto me, saying, [2]Son of man, cause Jerusalem to know her abo-mination ... [35]Wherefore, O harlot, hear the word of the LORD ... [48]As I live, saith the Lord GOD, Sodom thy sister hath not done, she nor her daughters, as thou hast done, thou and thy daughters" (Ezek. 16:1-2, 35, 48).

"[4] Hear Yahweh's word, O house of Jacob, and all the families of the house of Israel! ... [20] "For long ago I broke off your yoke, and burst your bonds. You said, 'I will not serve;' for on every high hill and under every green tree you bowed yourself, playing

24

the prostitute" (Jer. 2:4, 20).

"*6 Moreover, Yahweh said to me in the days of Josiah the king, "Have you seen that which back-sliding Israel has done? She has gone up on every high mountain and under every green tree, and has played the prostitute there*" (Jer. 3:6).

"*25 [j]Now this Hagar is mount Sinai in Arabia and answereth to the Jerusalem that now is: for she is in bondage with her children*" (Gal. 4:25).

The Book of Revelation gives us another clue regarding the "*woman (harlot)*" sitting upon the beast with seven heads and ten horns, which clearly predicts the apocalyptic fate of this great city:

"*16 And the ten horns which thou sawest, and the beast, these shall hate the harlot, and shall make her desolate and naked, and shall eat her flesh, and shall burn her utterly with fire*" (Rev. 17:3).

This verse corresponds to the geopolitical situation in the Middle East. Muslim countries hate Israel – Jerusalem is the heart of Israel. The beast that "*looks unto a leopard, and his feet were as the feet of a bear, and his mouth as the mouth of a lion*" represents the Muslim Empire. The "*ten horns*" that receive authority as kings, with the beast, for an hour must represent Muslim kings (kingdoms), as they rule with the beast (Rev. 17:12). Therefore, it is pertinent to suggest that "*ten horns*" could represent ten caliphates (kingdoms) within the Islamic Empire located predominantly on the territory of the former kingdoms prophetically described as "*leopard, bear, and lion.*" The "*beast*" and the "*ten horns*" cannot possibly hate Mecca, Istanbul, or any other city of their own; otherwise, it would lead to self-destruction. Jerusalem, however, is a different case: it represents Israel – Muslims hate Israel.

Some believers may argue that the verse "*woman whom thou sawest is that great city, which reigneth over the kings of the earth*" (Rev. 17:18) does not identify Jerusalem because, for the most part of its existence, this city was under the occupation of foreign rulers. That is true! Jerusalem has always been a desired trophy for many powerful leaders. However, the expression "*reigneth over the kings of the earth*" in this case should be understood in the spiritual sense. Jerusalem is the centre of three religions: Judaism, Christianity, and Islam. Here, the verse "*And the woman ... having in her hand a golden cup, [c] even the unclean things of her fornicationfull*" has spiritual significance. It symbolizes the great city that commits "*spiritual adultery*" by forsaking its spiritual purity, its allegiance to the God of Israel. Therefore, the expression "*harlot*" should be analyzed and interpreted in a spiritual sense.

Regardless of how devoted certain believers may be to Jerusalem and to the Old Testament, yet it is pertinent to affirm that after the crucifixion of the Messiah, that is to say, after the rejection of God's new covenant sealed by the blood of Jesus Christ, Jerusalem lost its divine glory. This statement is confirmed in the following Bible verses:

> "*[42] Jesus saith unto them, Did ye never read in the scriptures, [p] The stone which the builders rejected, The same was made the head of the corner; This was from the Lord, And it is marvellous in our eyes? [43] Therefore say I unto you, The kingdom of God shall be taken away from you, and shall be given to a nation bringing forth the fruits thereof. [44] [q] And he that falleth on this stone shall be broken to pieces: but on whomsoever it shall fall, it will scatter him as dust. [45] And when the chief priests and the Pharisees heard his parables, they perceived that he spake of them. [46] And when they sought to lay hold on him, they feared the*

multitudes, because they took him for a prophet" (Mt. 21:42-46).

"37 O Jerusalem, Jerusalem, that killeth the prophets, and stoneth them that are sent unto her! how often would I have gathered thy children together, even as a hen gathereth her chickens under her wings, and ye would not! 38 Behold, your house is left unto you [p]desolate. 39 For I say unto you, Ye shall not see me henceforth, till ye shall say, Blessed is he that cometh in the name of the Lord" (Mt. 23:37-39).

"And Jesus went out from the temple, and was going on his way; and his disciples came to him to show him the buildings of the temple. 2 But he answered and said unto them, See ye not all these things? verily I say unto you, There shall not be left here one stone upon another, that shall not be thrown down" (Mt. 24:1-2).

"34 O Jerusalem, Jerusalem, that killeth the prophets, and stoneth them that are sent unto her! how often would I have gathered thy children together, even as a hen gathereth her own brood under her wings, and ye would not! 35 Behold, your house is left unto you desolate: and I say unto you, Ye shall not see me, until ye shall say, Blessed is he that cometh in the name of the Lord" (Lk. 13:34-35).

"50 And Jesus cried again with a loud voice, and yielded up his spirit. 51 And behold, the veil of the [u] temple was rent in two from the top to the bottom; and the earth did quake; and the rocks were rent; 52 and the tombs were opened; and many bodies of the saints that had fallen asleep were raised; 53 and coming forth out of the tombs after his resurrection they entered into the holy city and appeared unto many. 54 Now the centurion, and they that were with him watching Jesus, when they saw the earthquake, and the things that were done, feared exceedingly, saying, Truly this was [v]the Son of God" (Mt. 27:50-54).

"37 And Jesus uttered a loud voice, and gave up the ghost. 38 And the veil of the [l]temple was rent in two from the top to the bottom. 39 And when the centurion, who stood by over against him, saw that he [m]so gave up the ghost, he said, Truly this man was [n]the Son of God" (Mk. 15:37-39).

"44 And it was now about the sixth hour, and a darkness came over the whole [g]land until the ninth hour, 45 [h]the sun's light failing: and the veil of the [i] temple was rent in the midst. 46 [j]And Jesus, crying with a loud voice, said, Father, into thy hands I commend my spirit: and having said this, he gave up the ghost. 47 And when the centurion saw what was done, he glorified God, saying, Certainly this was a righteous man" (Lk. 23:44-47).

It is said that, before the destruction of Jerusalem (in 70 AD), unusual things happened during religious services performed in the Temple, which were interpreted by some believers as a "sign" that the Glory of Yahweh left the Temple of Jerusalem. Indeed, God's Glory departed from the Temple! This has been confirmed by the destruction of Jerusalem and its religious edifice, and later by the Islamic mosque (with a full moon decoration on top of its dome, which evokes the crescent moon symbol of Islam) built on the place where once stood the famous Jewish Temple. Divine glory of God is revealed now to all those who accept the "word of God and keep the testimony of Jesus

Christ." This biblical reality is confirmed by Jesus Christ's statement in the following verses:

> "⁴² *Jesus saith unto them, Did ye never read in the scriptures,* [p]*The stone which the builders rejected, The same was made the head of the corner; This was from the Lord, And it is marvellous in our eyes?* ⁴³ *Therefore say I unto you, The kingdom of God shall be taken away from you, and shall be given to a nation bringing forth the fruits thereof*" (Mt. 21:42-43).

Nowadays, Jerusalem is the center of three major monotheistic religions: 1) Judaism, religion of the Old Testament; 2) Christianity, religion of the New Testament; 3) Islam, religion observing the Quran. All three contradict each other doctrinally, thus propagate a different version of God. Such doctrinal discordance reflects deviation from the truth, compromise. The Holy Spirit is not a spirit of compromise, but of truth, peace, and holiness.

Being destroyed as prophesied, and being under Roman pagan rule for several centuries and later under Muslim occupation for over twelve hundred years, the picture of Jerusalem nowadays doesn't seem to reflect the glory it once had, or the glory of the New Jerusalem described in Revelation chapter 21. Jerusalem is a city in grief, a shadow of what once used to be – it is rather a place of religious and political intrigues. Nowadays, one can see ancient ruins of what once was the greatness of Jerusalem. The real issue is not the original glory of Jerusalem (Mount Zion) but rather what this great city has become – a venue of religious and political events, which could trigger extreme violent reaction from its neighboring Islamic countries.

Jerusalem represents the heart of Judaism. This city is also the place where Jesus Christ was condemned to death by crucifixion, the place where initial persecution of Christians began. For believers under God's new covenant, the term "Jerusalem" has a new meaning. It is perceived as the "*spiritual Jerusalem*", that is, the "*new Jerusalem, coming down out of heaven from God*" – this is pointing towards the glorious return of our Lord Jesus Christ. How should a Christian believer identify himself with a city biblically described as " … *that killeth the prophets, and stoneth them that are sent unto her!*" (Mat. 23:37-38) and where ultimately the prophesied Messiah, Jesus Christ, was sentenced to death by "*crucifixion*"? Why do we see nowadays the "*Holy City*" in ruins? Was the destruction of Jerusalem and its Temple a fulfillment of biblical prophecy or a random incident? That is, should a reasonable believer consider the destruction of Jerusalem and the Temple, where the Roman army served as an instrument, a fulfillment of Jesus' prophecy or just a random military intervention of pagan Rome? Was Babylonian destruction of Jerusalem and the first Temple a fulfillment of Jeremiah's prophecy or just another historic incident? Isn't God, who inspires the prophets, in control of all these prophecies? Extra-biblical teachings and tendentious interpretations of the Bible are very dangerous weapons – a sad reality in religion.

Some believers will argue that such exegetical analysis is unacceptable because Jerusalem is the holiest place for Jews and Christians. However, those believers should not neglect one fact: the "*holiness*" of Jerusalem was due to the Ark of the Covenant, which stood in the Most Holy Place of the Temple, where the presence of Yahweh, the God of Israel, was manifested. Nowadays, one can see the ruins of what once was the holy edifice – undoubtedly, the consequence of Israel's disobedience and unfaithfulness to Yahweh. Believers under the new covenant are longing for a new city, the "*new Jerusalem coming down out of heaven from God*", described in Revelation chapter 21.

Observing ancestral traditions and deeming certain sites of Jerusalem as holy is very honourable – it is an expression of believer's faith and devotion to God. However, God does not dwell in man-made places (Is. 66:1; Acts 7:48-50). God is Spirit; His divine presence is manifested in the heart and mind of believers. And, just as God's chosen servants (prophets, apostles) have been sanctified by the Holy Spirit, in the same way a sanctuary or a site is sanctified by the presence of the same divine power. A physical object (a stone) as such does not sanctify. Therefore, if any religion promotes excess of zeal regarding the law and tradition, this often brings about unpredictable religious, social, and political consequences. In this case, exegetical reasoning regarding Jerusalem presented above would be inconsistent without clear biblical evidence; therefore, the following verses are indispensable:

> "*31 Behold, <u>the days come, says Yahweh, that I will make a new covenant with the house of Israel, and with the house of Judah</u>: 32 not according to the covenant that I made with their fathers in the day that I took them by the hand to bring them out of the land of Egypt; which my covenant they broke, although I was a husband to them, says Yahweh. 33 But <u>this is the covenant</u> that I will make with the house of Israel after those days, says Yahweh: <u>I will put my law in their</u> <u>inward parts, and in their heart will I write it</u>; and I will be their God, and they shall be my people*" (Jer. 31:31-33).

> "*21 Jesus saith unto her, Woman, believe me, <u>the hour cometh, when neither in this mountain, nor in Jerusalem, shall ye worship the Father</u>*" (Jn. 4:21).

> "*23 But <u>the hour cometh, and now is, when</u> <u>the</u> true worshippers shall worship the Father in spirit and truth</u>: [g]for such doth the Father seek to be his worshippers. 24 [h]<u>God is a Spirit: and they that worship him must worship in spirit and truth</u>*" (Jn. 4:23-24).

"[20] For <u>where two or three</u> are gathered together in my name, <u>there am I in the midst of them</u>" (Mt. 18:20).

"And I saw a new heaven and a new earth: for the first heaven and the first earth are passed away; and the sea is no more. 2 And <u>I saw [a]the holy city, new Jerusalem, coming down out of heaven from God</u>, made ready as a bride adorned for her husband" (Rev.21:1-2).

"[9] And there came one of the seven angels who had the seven bowls, who were laden with the seven last plagues; and he spake with me, saying, Come hither, <u>I will show thee the bride, the wife of the Lamb</u>. 10 And he carried me away in the Spirit to a mountain great and high, and <u>showed me the holy city Jerusalem, coming down out of heaven from God</u>" (Rev. 21:9-10).

An honest and devout believer, being under the guidance of the Holy Spirit, cannot say: biblical evidence quoted above is irrelevant. God is Spirit. The Holy Scripture is inspired by God, therefore, must be analysed in spirit and in truth. Those who seek the truth with a sincere heart will find it, and the truth will set them free.

Despite comprehensive analysis and convincing biblical evidence, there still is uncertainty regarding the identity of the "*woman (harlot).*" In this sense, Revelation 20:9 provides a conclusive clue:

"[7] And when the thousand years are finished, Satan shall be loosed out of his prison, 8 and shall come forth to deceive the nations which are in the four corners of the earth, Gog and Magog, to gather them together to the war: the number of whom is as the sand of the sea. 9 And <u>they</u> went up over the breadth of the earth, and <u>compassed the camp</u>

*of the saints about, and the beloved city: and fire
came down [e]out of heaven, and devoured them.
[10] And the devil that deceived them was cast into
the lake of fire and brimstone, where are also the
beast and the false prophet; and they shall be
tormented day and night [f]for ever and ever" (Rev.
20:7-9).*

This verse informs the reader that, before the end time, the
deceived nations will surround the *"camp of the saints, and the
beloved city"* – a reference to Jerusalem. This is a clear confir-
mation of the fact that the city of Jerusalem will stand even after
the destruction of the *"harlot (Babylon the Great)"*, after the
destruction of the beast and the false prophet. In this regard, it
is pertinent to affirm that Jerusalem cannot be the apocalyptic
"woman (harlot)" that sits upon the scarlet-coloured beast. The
initial persecution of Christians started in Jerusalem; however,
the verse *"woman drunken with the blood of the saints, and
with the blood of the martyrs of Jesus"* cannot prophetically
identify this religious city.

Prophetically, *"seven heads"* on which the woman sits are
"seven mountains" (Rev. 17:9); these are also *"seven kings"*
(Rev. 17:10). Heads or mountains represent *"waters"*, and
"peoples, and multitudes, and nations, and tongues" (Rev.
17:1, 15). Therefore, the *"woman (great city)"* sits or has
dominion over many kingdoms, peoples, and nations prophetically described as seven heads (mountains). The fact that in
prophetic language a *"mountain"* symbolizes a *"kingdom"* is
also confirmed in the Book of Daniel (Dan. 2:34-35, 44-45).
In reality, hills of Rome, Constantinople, Jerusalem, or any
other city are not kings or kingdoms – one cannot attribute to
a geographical "hill" such politico-administrative status. This
reasoning is confirmed by the following verses:

*"And there came one of the seven angels that had
the seven bowls, and spake with me, saying, Come*

hither, <u>I will show thee the judgment of the great harlot that sitteth upon many waters</u>" (Rev. 17:1).

"⁹ Here is the [i]mind that hath wisdom. <u>The seven heads are seven mountains</u>, on which the woman sitteth: ¹⁰ and [j]<u>they are seven kings; the five are fallen, the one is</u>, the other is not yet come; and when he cometh, he must continue a little while" (Rev. 17:9-10).

"¹⁵ And he saith unto me, <u>The waters which thou sawest, where the harlot sitteth, are peoples, and multitudes, and nations, and tongues</u>" (Rev. 17:15).

"¹⁸ And <u>the woman</u> whom thou sawest <u>is the great city</u>, which [k]reigneth over the kings of the earth" (Rev. 17:18).

The fact that seven mountains represent seven heads, seven kings (kingdoms), and also many waters (peoples, nations…) leads to the conclusion that the version according to which the *"woman (great city)"* sits on seven geographical hills is biblically contradictory. In this regard, it is pertinent to affirm that the beast with seven heads and ten horns represents an empire that has dominion over seven kingdoms (former empires) and at a definite time ten kings (kingdoms) rule within that empire – this beast represents the Muslim Empire; it is pertinent to assert that the *"woman (great city)"* in the wilderness that sits on a scarlet beast with seven heads and ten horns (Rev. 17:3) has to be an Islamic city; it is pertinent to assert that only an Islamic city can rule over the vast Islamic Empire. Mecca, the spiritual center of Islam, is the place where Muslim conquest commenced, which brought along many centuries of persecution and atrocities of non-Muslims throughout the conquered territory (Rev. 17:6). It is common sense to assert that Mecca, the heart of Islam, rules over the Muslim Empire. According to some critics, however, such assertion may be regarded as absurd because in the Book of Revelation is stated that the ten horns will destroy the woman (harlot) and burn her with fire (Rev. 17:16), therefore, how can ten Islamic horns hate and destroy Mecca, the most important Islamic city? Well, religious conflict between Shia and Sunni is reaching a critical point nowadays and the establishment of Islamic caliphate is destabilizing the Muslim world thus leading to unpredictable consequences. On the other hand, the prophecy tells us that the "*ten horns*", which will ultimately destroy the "*woman (great city)*" and burn her body with fire, fulfill God's will, and that "*ten horns*" agree and give their kingdom unto the beast until the word of God shall be fulfilled (Rev. 17:17). The following verses confirm this reasoning:

> "³ *And he carried me away in the Spirit into a wilderness: and I saw <u>a woman sitting upon a scarlet-colored beast</u>, [a]full of names of blasphemy, <u>having seven heads and ten horns</u>" (Rev. 17:3).*

> "⁶ *And I saw <u>the woman drunken with the blood</u> of <u>the saints, and with the blood of the [e]martyrs of Jesus</u>. And when I saw her, I wondered with a great wonder" (Rev. 17:6).*

> "¹⁶ *And <u>the ten horns</u> which thou sawest, <u>and the beast, these shall hate the harlot</u>, and shall make her desolate and naked, and shall eat her flesh, <u>and shall burn her utterly with fire</u>. ¹⁷ For <u>God did put in their hearts to do his mind</u>, and to come to one mind, and to give their kingdom unto the beast, <u>until the words of God should be accomplished</u>" (Rev. 17:16-17).*

> "²¹ *And [q]a strong angel took up a stone as it were a great millstone and cast it into the sea, saying, <u>Thus with a mighty fall shall Babylon, the great</u>*

city, be cast down, and shall be found no more at all" (Rev. 18:21).

Once again, the Holy Scripture teaches that "*seven heads*" on which the "*woman (harlot)*" sits are "*seven mountains*", that they are "*seven kings (kingdoms)*" (Rev. 17:9-10), and that the "*woman*" sits on many waters, which symbolize "*peoples, and multitudes, and nations, and tongues*" (Rev. 17:1, 15). The "*five fallen heads (kings)*" represent fallen empires of Babylonia, Medo-Persia, Greece, and quite probably Assyria and Egypt. According to the Book of Daniel, the third beast (Greek Empire), which extended its dominion over the territory of the previous empires (Medo-Persian and Babylonian), later was divided into four kingdoms prophetically described as "*four heads/horns*" (Dan. 7:6; 8:8). Three heads (horns) of the divided Greek Empire superposed kingdoms of Egypt, Assyria, Babylonia, and Medo-Persia.

The version according to which prophetic allegory "*his death-stroke was healed*" (Rev. 13:3) represents the revived Western Roman Empire and the "*little horn*", before which "*three of the first horns*" were plucked up by the roots, represents the Papacy, is based on Daniel 7:7-8. It is very evident that prophetic characteristics of the beast of Revelation chapters 13 and 17 are attributed to the fourth beast of Daniel chapter 7. This seems to be a very brave attempt to solve the prophecy; however, it is inconsistent and rather contradictory as follows:

1) According to Revelation chapter 13, the beast with seven heads and ten horns was "*like unto a leopard, and his feet were as the feet of a bear, and his mouth as the mouth of a lion*" – leopard, bear, and lion represent a prophetic allegory of the Greek, Medo-Persian, and Babylonian Empires. The Roman Empire is missing; therefore, the beast is not related to the Roman Empire. This beast is to be searched on the territory of kingdoms prophetically described as "*leopard, bear, and lion.*"

36

2) The version according to which "*ten horns*" represent ten European nations arising after the fall of the Western Roman Empire makes no sense, as prophetic allegory "*leopard, bear, and lion*" cannot be attributed to the Western Roman Empire.

3) According to Revelation chapter 17, the "*ten horns*" receive power as kings for one hour with the beast (Rev. 17:12). This beast prophetically described as "*was, and is not; and is about to come up out of the abyss*", and also as "*was, and is not, is himself also an eighth, and is of the seven*", is in fact one of the "*five are fallen.*" The Roman Empire, when John received prophetic visions of Revelation, was the sixth head, that is, "*one is*", not one of the five fallen heads (empires). Therefore, the "*beast that was, and is not, and is about to come*" and the "*ten horns*" cannot be attributed to the Roman Empire – the beast must be related to one of the empires that was before the Roman Empire.

4) If the "*beast with seven heads and ten horns*" described in Revelation chapters 13 and 17 cannot be attributed to the Roman Empire, and if the "*ten horns*" that receive power as kings for one hour with the beast cannot be attributed to West European nations coming out after the fall of the Western Roman Empire, then the "*little horn*", before which "*three of the first horns*" were plucked up by the roots (Dan. 7:8, 24), cannot be attributed to the Papacy, and the "*three uprooted horns*" cannot be three kings (kingdoms) coming out of the Western Roman Empire.

5) The following reasoning demonstrates that the beast of Revelation described as "*one of his heads as though it had been [b]smitten unto death; and his death-stroke was healed*" (Rev. 13:3), as "*was, and is not, and is obout come up out of the abyss*" (Rev. 17:8), and as "*was, and is not, is himself also an eighth, and is of the seven*" (Rev. 17:11) identifies an empire geographically located in the Middle East – it refers to the rise of Muslim Empire:

- Prophetic allegory *"feet part of iron, and part of clay"* (Dan. 2:33, 42) – the last empire of Nebuchadnezzar's prophetic statue – refer to the Islamic Empire, as it consisted partly of iron, the conquered Roman territory in the Middle East and North Africa, and partly of clay (earth, desert), the new territorial conquests in the Middle East, Central Asia, and African;

- Two prophetic allegories described in Revelation chapter 9 draw particular attention: the "<u>*pit of the abyss*</u>" and the "<u>*locusts*</u>" that came out of the smoke, which arose from the pit of the abyss. These locusts were commanded that *"they should not hurt the grass of the earth, neither any green thing, neither any tree, but only such men as have not the seal of God on their foreheads"* (Rev. 9:4). This is a clear proof that these are not ordinary locusts – a locust feeds on (green) vegetation. Desert locust invasion destroying crops is a reality in the Middle East and Africa. The Book of Joel chapter 2 describes desert locust invasion – a prophetic reference to a military invasion (an army). Therefore, it is very evident that the *"locusts"* of the Book of Revelation refer to a Muslim (Arab) army. On the other hand, the scarlet-coloured beast (Rev. 17:3, 8) also comes up out of the "<u>*abyss*</u>." Thus, the locusts and the beast with seven heads and ten horns have a similar prophetic characteristic – the two refer to the rise of one and the same empire;

- Muslims established their vast empire on the territory of the kingdoms prophetically described as *"leopard, bear, and lion"*, which geographically coincides with the Middle East;

- The verse *"And it was given unto him to make war with the saints, and to overcome them ..."* (Rev. 13:7) applies to Islamic Empire, as this is the empire that throughout its vast territory made war on Jews and Christians and defeated them. In this regard, it is pertinent to mention that similar prophetic characteristic is also attributed to the *"little horn"* described in Daniel (Dan. 7:8, <u>21</u>, 24-25) – this horn (king) seems to fit the beast of Revelation (Rev. 13:5-7), as the two have in common

similar prophetic characteristics. Although arguable, it is pertinent to suggest that the "*little horn (another king)*" refers to
the rise of Islamic Empire and the "*three horns plucked up by
the roots*" seem to correspond territorially to the three horns of
the divided Greek Empire, which to some extent were also part
of the Roman Empire;

- Bible verse "*These shall war against the Lamb . . .* "
(Rev. 17:14), where "*these*" refers to the ten horns, cannot
be attributed to ten Western European <u>Christian</u> nations.
However, the assertion that ten horns of the Islamic Empire
make war against the Lamb of God and His followers makes
sense – it is an undeniable biblical and hystorical reality.

6) It is very evident that apocalyptic beast with seven heads
and ten horns represents the Islamic Empire, which at its peak
stretched from the Atlantic coast of North Africa (and Iberian
Peninsula) to the Middle East and beyond. Therefore, "*ten
horns*" must be ten Muslim kings (kingdoms) ruling within the
Islamic Empire. In this sense, it is pertinent to suggest that "*ten
horns*" quite probably represent ten Islamic caliphates. History
confirms that the Muslim world was often governed by more
than one caliphate at the same period of time – parallel caliphates; on the other hand, smaller caliphates were conquered,
engulfed by the larger and more powerful ones. The issue
regarding caliphs and caliphates is debatable among Shia and
Sunni Muslims.

Any attempt to identify "*ten horns*" outside the Islamic
Empire does not concord with the following prophetic description: the beast looks like a "<u>*leopard, bear, and lion*</u>"; the beast
"<u>*was, is not, and is about to come up*</u>"; the ten horns "...<u>*receive
authority as kings, with the beast, for one hour*</u>." On the other
hand, prophetic expression "*receive authority as kings <u>for
one hour</u>*" is challenging. This seems to indicate a very short
time. Nevertheless, the beast with seven heads and ten horns,
also described as "<u>*an eighth, and is of the seven*</u>" (Rev. 17:11),

exercised its imperial authority during the reign of the horns ["...*on his horns ten diadems*" (Rev. 13:1) and "*ten horns (ten kings) ... receive authiority as kings, with the beast, for one hour*" (Rev. 17:12)], not during the reign of the heads. More than twelve centuries of Muslim imperial domination is not a short period of time. As the Islamic world is going through a severe crisis – the conflict between Shia and Sunni and the rise of Islamic Caliphate – it is reasonable to assert that ten horns of Islam, quite probably under the influence of the beast with "*two horns like unto a lamb*" (Rev 13:11) that exercises all the authority of the "*first beast in his sight*", are to rise and fulfill the prophecy of Revelation 17:16-17.

7) According to Revelation chapter 17, the scarlet beast with "*seven heads and ten horns*" ascends from the "*pit of the abyss*", not from the sea.

8) In the prophecy of Daniel is not mentioned the "*woman*" sitting upon the beast.

9) The verse "*And it was given unto him to make war with the saints, and to overcome them*" (Rev. 13:7; Dan. 7:21) seems ambiguous. Does it refer to Jews or Christians? If it refers only to the Jews – believers of the old covenant – then such interpretation reflects partiality because Christians – believers of the new covenant – are being excluded. If it refers to both Christians and Jews, to all those who honour God in spirit and in truth, then everything makes perfect sense. However, the Book of Revelation was revealed to John, a Christian, and is predominantly meant for believers under the new covenant, all those who accepted the "*word of God and the testimony of Jesus Christ*." For non-Christians, the Book of Revelation seems irrelevant! In the past, Muslims defeated Christians and Jews throughout the territory of the Islamic Empire. Even nowadays, persecution and acts of atrocity against Christian believers are still being committed in many Islamic countries.

10) Radical believers may argue that prophetic verse "*it was

given unto him to <u>make war with the saints, and to overcome them</u>" (Rev. 13:7; also Dan. 7:21) identifies imperial power of Rome manifested through destruction of Jerusalem, Crusades, Inquisition, and other military interventions of religious character. Indeed, the use of sword to solve religious conflicts is not in harmony with Christ's two commandment of (agape) love. Decision making is susceptible to human error; on the other hand, not all those involved in a just cause are sincerely devoted to their calling. Western society has been considerably influenced by double standard ideologies regarding the circumstances, causes, and provocations that triggered religious conflicts within Christianity. Roman siege and devastation of Jerusalem, which ended with the destruction of the Temple, and persecution of Christians in the first three centuries is a typical manifestation of pagan imperial power. The Crusades were military campaigns undertaken by Western Christians to free Jerusalem and the Holy Land, to defend Christianity from Muslim religious military aggression. However, Crusades had a limited success – Jerusalem and the Holy Land were re-conquered by Muslims. The Inquisition was created to combat heresy (according to canon law) and the spread of religious sectarianism. However, Protestant Reformation – the peak of anti-Catholicism – was not defeated. On the contrary, the Reformation spread all over the world. It is a known fact that, to some extent, Crusades and Inquisition were marked by human error and even departure from its original goal. Despite many differences of opinion, however, prophetic expression *"made war with saints, and overcame them"* cannot identify Christian Rome. Human history has many faces; quite often historical evidence is distorted, obscured, and history books dictated by the winners.

Despite clear biblical evidence, some critics may still deem exegetical analysis of the beasts of Revelation presented in this book as pro-Catholic, anti-Islamic. The answer to this remark is: such prophetic interpretation is pro-biblical and is confirmed by the Book of Revelation chapters 9, 13, 17, the Book of Daniel, and other biblical evidence. The given prophetic analysis comes in response to the following observation: How could "certain" historians, scholars, and religious leaders focus their attention mainly on Christianity and neglect or speak only vaguely of the beast ascending from the Middle East – the Muslim Empire – that made war on Jews and Christians and defeated them, the power that has been threatened Christianity with annihilation for many centuries? How could they focus their attention predominantly on Rome (and the alleged revived Western Roman Empire) thus ignore dramatic reality of Christians and Jews living in the Balkans, Middle East and other territories, ignore the undeniable fact that religious identity of those believers has been trampled upon for many centuries by Muslims? It is quite evident that such erroneous, tendentious interpretation of Bible prophecy is intended to divert believers' attention away from the truth.

History and religion have often been the subject of much speculation. Freedom of expression does not guarantee the veracity and accuracy of the facts, as an individual has the freedom of choice between speaking the truth or adopting a double standard position; therefore, this so-called "freedom" quite often becomes an instrument of propaganda and disinformation. Islam, the new religion that emerged in the 7th century, is ideologically antagonistic to Christianity and Judaism and, to a considerable extent, seems to counterfeit the Bible. According to traditional sources, Muslims initially were facing Jerusalem (the Temple Mount) during prayer; later, Muslim Qibla[6] (direction of prayer) was facing the Kaaba in Mecca. There seem to be interesting similarities between the Kaaba of the Great Mosque in Mecca and the Jewish Temple that stood in Jerusalem. Some of these similarities are: both cities are declare holy; both cities shelter the holiest site; both sites contain the holy stone; direction of worship; pilgrimage; circumambulation; animal sacrifices. Despite speculations over this issue, it seems that Kaaba of Mecca, from religious point of view, is an imitation of the Temple of Jerusalem. There are people who think that Islam is a religion of peace; however, they seem to manifest ignorance of history regarding persecution and atrocities committed for many centuries by Muslims and of the fact that thousands of Christian churches were destroyed or turned into mosques.

Islamic Empire lost its imperial dominion following the collapse of the Ottoman Caliphate; therefore, it seems that the beast with seven heads and ten horns has fallen. Nowadays, Islamic Empire as such no longer exists; however, its dominion throughout the territory of its former empire is manifested in a different form – <u>a religious Islamic form</u>. This new form of dominion seems to fit the beast prophetically described as "*coming up out of the earth…exerciseth all the authority of the first beast in his sight*" (Rev. 13:11-12). The complexity of this prophetic mystery is evident and certain questions still remain unanswered:

- Who is the seventh head, which prophetically is also described as "*when he cometh, <u>he must continue a little while</u>*" (Rev. 17:10)? The Hunnic Empire seems to identify with the seventh head. In the 5th century, this empire stretched from the steppes of Central Asia to Central Europe; however, it was a short lived empire – it lasted less than a century. Hunnic expansion stimulated the Great Migration (Barbarian Invasion); Huns also invaded Roman territory in Balkans and Central Europe. These two factors undoubtedly contributed to the collapse of the Western Roman Empire. On the other hand, the Mongol Empire could also be identified with this prophecy. This empire stretched from the Sea of Japan to Central Europe (including a considerable territory of the Middle East). At the zenith of its power, the empire was divided into four khanates, three of which adopted Islam – the religion of the beast (empire) that was already in the world for about six centuries; therefore, the Mongol Empire does not correspond to this prophecy. The Ottoman Empire cannot be the "*seventh head*", as its imperial dominion lasted 600 years (a long period of time) and was an Islamic caliphate;

- Who is the deadly wounded head whose deadly wound was healed? Was it one of the empires that preceded the Roman Empire? Was it the fatal wound of the Abbasid Caliphate in 1258, when Bagdad – the splendor of Islam at that time – was destroyed by the Mongols? According to the Book of Revelation chapter 17, the head that "*was, and is not*" is one of the "*five fallen heads.*" More precisely, this head (or the deadly wounded head) is the eighth king, the beast (Rev. 17:9-11) – it revives one of the fallen empires;

- Who are the ten horns, which receive authority as kings, with the beast, for one hour? It is quite evident that these horns must represent ten Muslim kings. These "*ten horns*" and the beast will hate the "*woman (great harlot)*" and ultimately destroy her and burn her with fire, thus fulfil the final act of Bible prophecy.

As mentioned previously, it is pertinent to attribute prophetic allegory the "*beast that looks like a leopard, bear, and lion*" to the Islamic Empire, as this empire geographically was located on the territory of kingdoms prophetically described as "*leopard, bear, and lion*", which represent the former Greek, Medo-Persian, and Babylonian empires. The Muslim Empire carved its way through history for more that twelve hundred years but no longer exists as such. However, we are witnessing Muslim religious aggressive expansion in various parts of the world, which quite often is manifested in a militaristic form.

Some believers consider that prophetic events described in the Book of Revelation have already taken place in the first century. Such approach of Bible prophecy, however, does not seem to provide a very consistent explanation regarding the identity of the beast that looks like "*leopard, bear, and lion*" (Rev. 13:2), the ten horns which are "*ten kings, which have received no kingdom as yet*" (Rev. 17:12), and the beast with "*two horns like a lamb*" (Rev. 13:11). On the other hand, the rise of Muslim Empire and other subsequent events of prophetic and historic significance do not seem to be part of the Apocalypse anymore.

In summary, the following conclusive remarks regarding the identity of the beast with seven heads and ten horns deserve due consideration:

1) The allegations according to which prophetic allegory "*smitten unto death head*" refers to the historic event that took place in 476 and the prophecy regarding the "*end of the 1260 evenings and mornings*" was fulfiled in 1798 are contradictory.

2) The beast with seven heads and ten horns described as "*was like unto a leopard, and his feet were as the feet of a bear, and his mouth as the mouth of a lion*", and as "*was, and is not, and is about to come*" cannot be attributed to the Western Roman Empire in any form.

3) Several Protestant reformers propagated, among other things, the teaching according to which the Papacy (the Pope) was identified as the beast, the Antichrist. Therefore, it is quite evident that many Christians during the Protestant Reformation had been caught in a very aggressive religious propaganda campaign, which consequently contributed to the escalation of religious conflicts and bloodshed between Catholics and Protestants. In this regard, prophetic allegations of those reformers were inconsistent and contradictory, as the beasts of Revelation described in chapter 13 and 17 cannot be attributed to the Western Roman Empire. Therefore, no matter whether it

was erroneous or tendentious, such distorted interpretation of Bible prophecy cannot be regarded as the "*Sola Scriptura (by Scripture alone)*."

Prophetic mysteries of the Book of Revelation have always been the subject of constant speculation. Therefore, brief exegetical analysis of the beasts of Revelation presented in this book will not be exempt from speculative comments. However, one thing should be very clear to the reader: the identity of this prophetic beast is to be searched on the territory where once empires prophetically described as "*leopard, bear, and lion*" were located – this is predominantly the Middle East territory, the Muslim countries. Any attempt to identify the beast with seven heads and ten horns elsewhere is futile.

> "[32] *and ye shall know the truth, and the truth shall make you free*" (Jn. 8:32).

The beast with two horns like a lamb

> *"[11] And I saw another beast coming up out of the earth; and he had two horns like unto a lamb, and he spake as a dragon. [12] And he exerciseth all the authority of the first beast in his sight. And he maketh the earth and them that dwell therein to [m]worship the first beast, whose death-stroke was healed" (Rev. 13:11-12).*

The second beast of the Book of Revelation is described as coming out of the earth and is as sinister as the first one. There are several interpretations regarding the identity of this apocalyptic beast. Some of these commentaries undoubtedly manifest a sincere intent to solve this centuries-long prophetic dilemma; others, however, prove to be rather speculations or tendentious interpretations.

According to some scholars, this prophetic beast represents the United States of America; others consider that it has to do with Europe; yet there are those who believe that it is none of the two. Consequently, biblical message of this prophecy is obscured and discord among believers continues.

This beast (empire) has certain particularities:

- "*he had <u>two horns</u> like a lamb*" (Rev. 13:11). Horns of a lamb are small, inoffensive. The lamb symbolizes innocence, purity, and biblically was used in religious rituals. Therefore, "*two horns like a lamb*" must refer to a religion-based empire;

- "*he spoke as a dragon*" (Rev. 13:11). This means that the beast was involved in religious wars and used arrogant religious claims;

- "*exercises all the authority of the first beast <u>in his sight</u>*" (Rev. 13:12). **Note:** Some Bible versions contain: "*. . . on his behalf . . .*" instead of "*. . . <u>in his sight</u> (or in his presence) . . .*" (Rev. 13:12) – a rather controversial translation;

- makes the earth and its inhabitants "*worship the first beast, whose death-stroke was healed*" (Rev. 13:12);

- makes all, the small and the great, and the rich and the poor, and the free and the bond, that "<u>*there be given them a mark on their right hand, or upon their forehead*</u>" (Rev. 13:16);

- no man should be able to buy or to sell unless he has the "<u>*the mark, even the name of the beast or the number of his name*</u>" (Rev. 13:17);

- the number of the beast is a number of a man: its number is "<u>*Six hundred and sixty six*</u>." The issue regarding the "*name or the number of the beast*", which identifies the first beast, is quite debatable. According to Bible scholars, the following names could identify with this mystery number (666): Nero Caesar, Vicarius Filli Dei (allegedly once a title of the Pope), Muhammad, and so on. Nevertheless, the Bible gives us a clue: the mark represents the "*number of his name*", <u>not</u> the number of his <u>title</u>.

At first impression, there is no doubt that such prophetic language is a mystery. What does prophetic beast with two horns like a lamb represent? Why is the beast coming out of the earth? There is a similarity between prophetic expressions "*earth*" and "*abyss*", does it convey a message? How does this beast make the nations worship the first beast, whose deadly wound was healed? What is the name or the number of the beast? It is not an easy task to solve such a complex prophetic enigma.

Despite these prophetic challenges, the Holy Scripture always provides clues to solving biblical mysteries. It is the moral duty of believers under the guidance of the Holy Spirit to use and interpret these clues properly.

Version 1

Some believers are being indoctrinated with the teaching that the "*beast with two horns like a lamb*" represents the United States of America, and that the "*two horns*" represent two principles or freedoms (religious and political) on which this new country was established. Some venture to say that the two horns represent two American political parties (republican and democrat).

Let's see what the spirit of prophecy has to say about this matter. The Bible states very clearly that a "*horn*" represents a "*king or kingdom*" (Dan. 7:24; Dan. 8:20-22; Rev. 17:12), not principles or freedoms.

According to the Book of Revelation, the second beast exercises "*all the authority of the first beast in his sight*" and makes inhabitants of the earth to worship the "*first beast, whose death-stroke was healed*" (Rev. 13:12). The expression "*in his sight*" means that the notion of space is irrelevant, as the second beast exercises all the power of the first beast in his sight (in his presence). Therefore, it would be nonsense to assert that the "*first beast*" is in Europe and the "*second beast*" is on the other side of Atlantic Ocean, in America. In other words, this version lacks consistency thus is not in concordance with Bible prophecy.

In the U.S. Constitution, the words "God, Jesus Christ, Christianity, Bible" are not mentioned, therefore, giving the impression that it was not founded on Christianity – it seems rather a secular document. Some people may argue that this was done with the intention to maintain the so-called religious neutrality. Furthermore, in the Declaration of Independence of the United States[7] are stated, among other things, the following: "the Laws of Nature and of Nature's God" and "endowed by their Creator." Such statements, however, reflect rather a deistic viewpoint. Can the USA, allegedly the second beast, be identified as "exercising the power of the first beast" whose deadly wound was healed, allegedly the revived Western Roman Empire (a Christian empire)? No!

These believers have been also indoctrinated with the teaching that the number of the beast "*666*" (Rev. 13:18) represents the Pope. According to such logic, the second beast is located in the USA and the number of the beast, that is, the first beast is located in Vatican (Europe); therefore, two authorities with radically different ideologies in two different locations separated by an ocean. This prophetic interpretation is erroneous – it contradicts prophetic statement "*exerciseth all the authority of the first beast in his sight*" (Rev. 13:12). It is quite evident that such a contradictory interpretation of Bible prophecy is not just faulty but also tendentious.

Version 2

It is quite tempting for some believers to assert that this prophetic beast could represent the divided Roman Empire, the Eastern and Western Roman Empire. The following arguments corroborate this version:

- the two horns represent two emperors ruling this divided empire: 1) the emperor of the Western Roman Empire ruling from Rome; 2) the emperor of the Eastern Roman (Byzantine) Empire ruling from Constantinople;

- horns like a lamb are small, inoffensive. The lamb symbolizes innocence, purity, and biblically was used in religious rituals. Therefore, "*two horns like a lamb*" refer to a religion-based empire: 1) Eastern Byzantine (Orthodox); 2) Western Roman Catholic;

- this divided empire was involved in religious wars and persecution of believers. Despite the fact that it had been ruled by Christian emperors and Christian religion became its official religion, yet this empire (beast) exercised the vast political, military, judicial, and administrative authority of the first beast (the vast authority of the pagan Roman Empire); therefore, it spoke like a dragon.

Some skeptical believers allege that the "*mark on the right hand, or on the forehead*" has something to do with the practice in religious services, ceremonies, and prayers where right hand and forehead are involved – they seem to view the sign of the cross as a practice that has no biblical support, an idolatry. Such a provocative allegation nourishes an anti-Christian spirit, therefore, requires a categorical response: The cross – a symbol of Christianity – represents the instrument on which Jesus Christ was crucified. On the cross of Golgotha, Christ established God's new covenant with His people (Lk. 22:19-20; Mt. 26:26-28; 1Cor. 11:24-25). The cross is a symbol of our redemption in Christ, a symbol of Christ's victory over sin and death. The sign of the cross is a ritual blessing practiced in the Catholic and Orthodox Churches; it is also practiced in Anglican, Lutheran, and to some extent in Methodist and Reformed (Calvinist) Churches. The first historic evidence of use of the sign of the cross by Christians seems to date back to the 2nd century AD – at that time the Roman Empire was not divided. Therefore, it is very evident that the "*sign of the cross*" cannot be offensive to God; the cross as a symbol of Christianity – the religion of God's new covenant – cannot represent the mark of the beast.

No matter how plausible the arguments in favour of this version may be, a vital prophetic fact must not be neglected: the second beast "<u>*exerciseth all the authority of the first beast in his sigh*</u>" and makes inhabitants of the earth to "*worship the first beast, whose death-stroke was healed*" (Rev. 13:12). Therefore, the second beast uses the vast authority of the first beast in its presence, that is, in the presence of the beast prophetically described as "*was like unto a <u>leopard</u>, and his feet were as the feet of a <u>bear</u>, and his mouth as the mouth of a* *lion*" (Rev. 13:2). According to the Book of Daniel, "*leopard, bear, and lion*" represent three ancient empires (Greek, Medo-Persian, and Babylonian). Therefore, the second beast must be also searched on the territory where empires described as "*leopard, bear, and lion*" were once located, which is predominantly the territory of the Middle East – the Muslim countries nowadays. The Roman Empire has never been prophetically described as "*leopard, bear, and lion*"; therefore, the allegation that divided Eastern and Western Roman Empire exercising the authority of the beast that looked like a "*leopard, bear, and lion*", which cannot be atributed to the Roman Empire, is absolute nonsense. The divided Roman Empire cannot identify with prophetic beast with two horns like a lamb.

Version 3

Despite many conflicts and religious divergences within Christianity, it would be unreasonable to neglect the rise of the new empire in the Middle East, which, by putting an end to the Byzantine Empire, became an imminent threat to the entire Christianity. It is not right to overlook the means by which it became an empire – use of the sword (in the name of Allah). It isn't correct to neglect many Muslim attempts to conquer Western Europe (Western Christianity). It is unreasonable to concentrate only on the speck in the eye of Christianity and neglect the log in the eye of Islam. The real issue here is that prophetic message of the Book of Revelation is much more than what some of us were taught to believe, much more than what certain scholars, historians, and politicians would want us to accept.

As mentioned before, the beast with seven heads and ten horns prophetically described as "*was like unto a leopard, and his feet were as the feet of a bear, and his mouth as the mouth of a lion*" (Rev. 13:1-2), where the (iron) Roman

Empire is missing, confirms the fact that the identity of this beast is related somehow to the former Greek, Medo-Persian, and Babylonian Empires. In other words, this empire (beast) comprises the territory of the Balkan Peninsula and the Middle East, that is to say, it stretches from the fertile Balkan territory towards the desert, towards the abyss (Rev. 13:1-2; Rev. 17:3, 8; Rev. 9:1-3, 11).

In Revelation chapter 17, the scarlet-coloured beast (in the wilderness) with seven heads and ten horns – the "*eighth king* (*the beast*)" – is described as "is *about* <u>*to come up out of the abyss*</u>" (Rev. 17:3, 8). In Revelation chapter 13, the second beast is described as "<u>*coming up out of the earth*</u>" (Rev. 13:11). Prophetic expressions "*earth*, abyss, *wilderness (desert)*" are synonymous, thus have a common characteristic – this implies similarity regarding the nature and origin of the beasts.

The second beast had "<u>*two horns like a lamb*</u>, *and he spake as a dragon.*" How big the horns of a lamb can be? Why harmless horns of a lamb? Perhaps, the spirit of prophecy intends to associate "*horns as a lamb*" with "*horns as a ram*"? According to the Book of Daniel, the "*ram with two horns*" represents Medo-Persian Empire (Dan. 8:1-3, 20).

What do the "*two horns like a lamb*" represent? Some believers identify the "*two horns*" with Shia and Sunni – the two major branches of Islam, which also represent two Islamic religious leaders; others consider that this prophecy is yet to be fulfilled. However, regardless of what the "*two horns*" represent, these are related to the Middle East, as the beast with two horns "<u>*exerciseth all the authority of the first beas in his sight*</u>", that is, the second beast exercises all the authority of the first beast that "*was unto a <u>leopard</u>, and his feet were as the feet of a <u>bear</u>, and his mouth as the mouth of a <u>lion</u>*" in its presence.

Once again, as the beast with seven heads and ten horns looked like "<u>*a leopard, a bear, and a lion*</u>", it is common sense to focus our search for the identity of the beast with "*two horns like a lamb*", which exercises all the power of the first beast <u>in his sight</u>, on the territory where the empires allegorically described as "*leopard, bear, and lion*" were once located.

Searching for the beast that looks like a "*leopard, bear, and lion*" in Western Europe, that is, within the Western Christianity is prophetically contradictory; searching for the beast with "*two horns like a lamb that spoke as a dragon*" on territory other than the Middle East – the Muslim countries – is futile. Can prophetic allegory "*spake as a dragon*" apply to a Christian kingdom that has accepted the "*word of God and the testimony of Jesus Christ*"? No! Nevertheless, certain scholars chose to ignore the rise of Islamic Arab Empire that made its way through with the use of the sword. Somehow, they chose to focus their search within Christianity. Is there a particular reason for that? Yes, it is quite evident!

Amazing scientific breakthroughs in last several decades are astonishing. However, the version according to which the "*mark of the beast*" is an implant of microchip "*on the right hand, or on the forehead*" is a <u>diversion</u>. Its principal scope is to hinder believers from realizing that this prophecy is unfolding now. It would be very naive on the part of Christians to uphold the idea that believers' salvation or condemnation does not depend on their faith, but on a microchip implant. Why only on the right hand or on forehead? Why not on other parts of the body as well? Note that the "*mark of the beast*" represents the "*name of the beast or the number of his name*" (Rev. 13:17). What is the logic of imposing a microchip implant (containing someone's name) on people's right hand or forehead? Prophetically, the "*mark*" represents the name of the beast or the number of its name (Rev. 13:17-18). What does the alleged microchip (mark) represent?

The "*beast*" is in total opposition and rebellion against God. Acceptance or rejection of the "*mark of the beast*" involves people's faith, their religion. Therefore, this issue is of religious nature, as the beast "*makes the earth and them that dwell therein <u>to worship the first beast</u>, whose death-stroke was healed*", as the first beast "*opened his mouth for blasphemies against God, to blaspheme his name, and his tabernacle*", and as it was given unto him "*to make war with the saints, and to overcome them.*" This statement is confirmed by the following Bible verses:

"*5 and there <u>was given to him a mouth speaking great things and blasphemies</u>; and there was given to him authority [e]to continue forty and two months. 6 And <u>he opened his mouth for blasphemies against God, to blaspheme his name, and his tabernacle</u>, even them that [f]dwell in the heaven. 7 [g]And it was given unto him to make war with the saints, and to overcome them: and there was given to him authority over every tribe and people and tongue and nation.*" (Rev. 13:5-7)

"*12 And <u>he exerciseth all the authority of the first beast in his sight</u>. And he maketh the earth and them that dwell therein to [m]worship the first beast, whose death-stroke was healed*" (Rev. 13:12).

"*15 And <u>it was given unto him to give breath to it, even to the image of the beast, [n]that the image of the beast should both speak, and cause</u> that as many as should not [o]worship the image of the beast should <u>be killed</u>*" (Rev. 13:15).

"*9 And another angel, a third, followed them, saying with a great voice, <u>If any man [d]worshippeth the beast and his image, and receiveth a mark on his forehead, or upon his hand, 10 he also shall drink of the wine of the wrath of God</u>, which is [e] prepared unmixed in the cup of his anger; and he*

*shall be tormented with fire and brimstone in the
presence of the holy angels, and in the presence of
the Lamb: [11] and the smoke of their torment goeth
up [f]for ever and ever; and <u>they have no rest day
and night, they that [g]worship the beast and his
image, and whoso receiveth the mark of his name</u>.
[12] Here is the [h]patience of the saints, they that
keep the commandments of God, and the faith of
Jesus"* (Rev. 14:9-12).

The controversy over the "*mark of the beast*" has been going on
for many centuries. Certain believers allege that Sunday, that is,
Sunday keeping represents the mark of the beast (and Sabbath
is the seal of God). This, however, demonstrates lack of logical
reasoning – a typical product of spiritually abusive indoctrina-
tion – as follows:

- According to their logic, all Christians who have been
keeping Sunday for almost two millenniums have the mark of
the beast;

- Jesus Christ was resurrected on Sunday, the first day of
the week (Mt. 28:1-7; Mk. 16:1-7; Lk. 24:1-7; Jn. 20:1-9);
Jesus revealed Himself to His disciples on Sunday (Mt. 28:1-
17; Mk. 16:9-14; Lk. 24:13-35; Jn. 20:11-29); the Holy Spirit
descended upon the apostles and other followers of Christ on
Sunday (Acts 2:1-4; Lev. 23:15-16); first-century Christians
were gathering for worship, prayer, and the Holy Communion
on Sunday, the first day of the week (Acts 20:7; 1Cor. 11:17-22;
1Cor. 16:1-2). Do all the above mentioned [Christ's resurrection, Pentecost (descent of the Holy Spirit), Christian gathering for worship on Sunday] imply the acceptance of the mark
of the beast, that is, worshiping the beast? No! Such allegation
is a blasphemous;

- Jewish religious leaders were plotting to kill Jesus for
breaking the Sabbath law; therefore, the alleged Sabbath
breaking was one of the three main accusations, which led to

Jesus' arrest and ultimately to His death by crucifixion (Mt. 12:9-14; Mk. 3:1-6; Lk. 13:10-14; Jn. 5:17-18; Jn. 9:15-16; Mt. 12:1-2);

- Seventh-day Sabbath is never described in the Bible as the seal of God – the Sabbath represents a sign of the covenant between Yahweh and the people liberated from Egyptian slavery (Ex. 31:13, 16). On the other hand, the Bible states very clearly that the seal of God is manifested by the presence of the Holy Spirit within believer's life (Eph. 1:13; Eph. 4:30; 2Cor. 1:21-22);

- The Bible provides clear evidence that God put an end to the old covenant (Jer. 31:31-33; Heb. 8:7-13; Mt. 26:26-27; Mk. 14:22-24; Lk. 22:19-20; 1Cor. 11:23-25) and to the seventh-day Sabbath (Is. 1:13; Hos. 2:11; Col. 2:14-17; Gal. 4:9-11; Eph. 2:14-15; Mk. 2:27-28; Mt. 11:28). This has been achieved on the cross of Golgotha through Jesus Christ. Both the old covenant established on Mount Sinai and seventh-day Sabbath are interconnected; therefore, if God put an end to the old covenant, He also put an end to seventh-day Sabbath, the sigh of that covenant. The law, the basis of the old covenant, was in charge of the people to lead them to Christ that they may be justified by faith (Ex. 34:27-28; Gal. 3:24-25; 2Cor. 3:6). Believers under the new covenant keep Christ's two commandments of love (agape) on which the entire law and the prophets depend (Mat. 22:36-40);

- If some believers still consider seventh-day Sabbath an everlasting sign (Ex. 31:13, 16), then they should observe all other practices and requirements declared as everlasting by the Old Testament law. They should apply within their communities the death penalty for breaking the Sabbath, as required by the law (Ex. 31:14-15). How many of them would pass this test nowadays? They should also observe the Sabbath year (Lev. 23:3-5; Ex. 23:10-11);

- We rest whenever we feel tired, exhausted. True rest

(worship), that is, true Sabbath is in spirit. We have that rest in Christ and through Christ (Jn. 4:24; Mt. 11:28; Jn. 14:6).

Ultimately, what does the beast with two horns like a lamb represent? Where is it located? The answer to these questions is found in the following verse:

> "*12 And he exerciseth all the authority of the first beast in his sight. And he maketh the earth and them that dwell therein to [m]worship the first beast, whose death-stroke was healed" (Rev. 13:12).*

The second beast is located on the territory of the first beast, which in prophetic language looks like a "*leopard, bear, and lion*" – the Middle East territory. As we already know, the first beast corresponds to the rise of Islamic Empire. This empire has a certain particularity: its military conquests have been motivated by its religious ambitions – in the name of Allah. However, this empire disintegrated politically and militarily after the fall of the Ottoman Caliphate (Empire).

Nowadays, the Islamic Empire as such no longer exists; however, all Islamized nations that once constituted the Islamic Empire have in common one vital characteristic: they all share Islamic religion – the nucleus of the Islamic Empire. Thus, all these countries are united in Islam, the religion of the former Islamic Empire. Nowadays, even though we do not see Muslim military expansion as in the past, yet there are various forms of Muslim religious aggression, which prophetically are described as "*spake as a dragon.*" Therefore, nowadays we see a new empire – a religious form empire – that "*exerciseth all the authority of the first beast in his sight*", that is, this new beast exercises all the power of the first beast – its power has its source in the Islamic religion of the first beast. The two horns seem to represent two religious leaders, the so-called two successors of their prophet Muhammad, which also stand for Shia and Sunni – the two major denominations of Islam. It is not a secret that, for a long time, radical Muslims have been propagating the idea of restoring the Islamic Caliphate and promoting the teaching that Islam will dominate the world. Nowadays, the world is witnessing an apocalyptic event: the reinstatement of Islamic caliphate in the Middle East.

For many centuries, transgression of Sharia law – the moral code and religious law of Islam – was punished with death penalty. From the earliest history of Islam, apostasy was punished with death penalty. Apostasy in Islam includes: abandonment of Islam by a Muslim, converting to another religion, speaking against Allah, Quran, Muhammad, and so on. Nowadays, it is no secret that some Islamic countries still practice the capital punishment for breaking certain Sharia laws. Could Sharia law represent prophetic allegory "*the image of the beast should both speak, and cause that as many as should not [o]worship the image of the beast should be killed*" (Rev. 13:14-15)? This is a very sensitive topic! However, such controversial practices are not something new to the mankind: according to the Old Testament, transgression of certain Mosaic laws was also punished with death penalty. On the other hand, besides Sharia law, Muslims also have their own Islamic calendar (Hijri calendar)[8] according to which the year AD 622 becomes the first year of the Muslim calendar. Could this be a reference to the prophecy "*He shall think to change times and laws*" (Dan. 7:25)?

As a suggestion, the moral duty of Christians is to live a holy life and be always prepared for the return of our Lord Jesus Christ – they should not be fanatically obsessed with the identity of these apocalyptic beasts. A Christian should avoid futile and spiritually unconstructive arguments.

In conclusion, this brief exegetical analysis of the beasts of Revelation, substantiated by incontestable biblical evidence, confirms the fact that the "*beast with two horns like a lamb*" is related to the Middle East, not to the North America or

Europe as some scholars allege. This commentary is not intended to offend any religion or people's faith. It should not be regarded as an attack on Islam, but rather a revelation of certain prophetic truth described in the Book of Revelation, which is ignored by Muslims. It has nothing to do with politics or the Middle East crisis. The art of compromise called politics and the true worship of God are two radically different things – God does not condone compromise. The purpose of this analytical reasoning is to shed a new light on the understanding of prophetic allegory "*the beast with two horns like a lamb*" and demonstrate that several current interpretations of this prophecy are erroneous or tendentious, thus not in harmony with the word of God.

> "[32] *and ye shall know the truth, and the truth shall make you free*" (Jn. 8:32).

Conclusion

God's divine attributes are clearly seen throughout the universe. The Bible is God's written revelation of His will to humankind. Most Bible revelations are quite comprehensible to the average mind; however, prophetic visions presented in symbolic language make an exception.

Devout believers have always been intrigued by the prophetic mysteries of the Bible. Believers, who give proper consideration to prophetic messages delivered by the prophets, enjoy God's blessing; those who neglect them, suffered the consequence of disobedience. However, sporadic appearance of false prophets spreading false teachings, thus bringing about confusion and rebellion among believers, is a reality biblically confirmed. Christianity is not exempt from false prophets and false interpretations of the word of God; Christians, according to the New Testament, are being warned of such danger.

Erroneous or tendentious interpretations of Bible prophecy have a powerful effect on the human mind. People's ignorance of the Scripture and of historical facts, their naivety in trusting human reason more than the word of God hinders them from realizing the deception engulfing them. Being deceived or seduced into accepting false ideologies, such believers become subject to doctrinal manipulation and consequently deviate from the "*word of God.*"

Exegetical analysis regarding the identity of the beasts of Revelation presented in this book concludes with the following remarks:

- The red dragon and the beast with seven heads and ten horns represent Satan's dominion exercised through succession of earthly powers (empires);
- The beast that "*was like unto a <u>leopard</u>, and his feet were*

as the feet of a <u>bear</u>, and his mouth as the mouth of a <u>lion</u>" is to be searched on the territory where once empires prophetically described as *"leopard, bear, and lion"* were located. This prophetic beast identifies the rise of Islamic Empire. Its vast empire was established on the territory of the former empires of Greece, Medo-Persia, and Babylonia;

- The Roman Empire was never prophetically describe as *"leopard, bears, and lion"*; therefore, the beast with seven heads and ten horns, which was *"like unto a <u>leopard</u>, and his feet were as the feet of a <u>bear</u>, and his mouth as the mouth of a <u>lion</u>"* cannot be attributed to the Roman Empire, in particular, the Western Roman Empire;

- The version according to which *"ten horns"* ascended from the Western Roman Empire is unreasonable, as prophetic description *"leopard, bear, and lion"* cannot be attributed to that empire;

- The *"ten horns"* that came out of the Roman Empire (Dan. 7:24), to a considerable extent, are related to the collapsed Eastern Roman Empire (Byzantine Empire);

- It is pertinent to attribute prophetic allegory *"ten horns"* to Muslim kings/kingdoms (caliphates), as these were located on territories of the former empires of leopard (Greece), bear (Medo-Persia), and lion (Babylonia). It is reasonable to assert that the *"ten horns"*, which receive power as kings with the beast prophetically also described as *"was, and is not"* (when John received the Revelation), cannot be related to the Roman Empire;

- Prophetically, the Roman Empire identifies with the sixth head, the *"one is"* (Rev. 17:10), thus cannot be one of the *"five are fallen."* Therefore, prophetic allegory *"the beast that was, and is not…"* (Rev. 17:11) cannot be attributed to the Roman Empire in any form, and the *"ten horns"* cannot be attributed to the so-called revived Western Roman Empire;

- Prophetic allegory *"feet part of iron, and part of clay"*

(Dan. 2:33, 42) refers to the Islamic Empire, as it consisted partly of territory once appertaining to the Eastern Roman Empire (iron) and partly of non-Roman territory (clay, desert), that is, partly the conquered Roman territory in the Middle East, North Africa, Balkans and partly the conquered territories beyond the border of the Roman Empire (South Central Asia and new territories in Africa);

- It is pertinent to attribute prophetic expressions "*in the wilderness (desert)*" and "*is about to come up out of the abyss*" (Rev. 17:3, 8) to the rise of Islamic Empire, as Islam originated in the Arabian Peninsula, which is predominantly a desert territory (wilderness);

- It is correct to attribute the "*42 months*" prophecy (Rev. 11:2-3; also Rev. 13:5), that is, 1260 days or 1260 years (according to "day-year" principle) to the Islamic Empire, as this was the only military power that occupied Jerusalem (the holy city) for more than 12 centuries;

- The beast with seven heads and ten horns described in the Book of Revelation chapters 13 and 17 represents one and the same beast at two different stages (incipient and final) of its existance [**Note** the similarity: "*all that dwell on earth…whose name has not been writen in the book of life* … *" (Rev.13:8; Rev.17:8)]. This beast refers to one and the same head: "*his death-stroke was healed*" (Rev. 13:3, 12); "*was, and is not; and is about to come up*" (Rev. 17:8, 11); "*is himself also an eighth, and is of the seven*" (Rev. 17:11). It also refers to the time of reign of the ten horns: "on his horns *ten diadems*" (Rev. 13:1); "*ten horns…receive authority as kings, with the beast, for one hour*" (Rev. 17:12). Therefore, contrary to many faulty interpretations, it is more appropriate to say: <u>one head with ten horns</u> (Rev. 17:12), not seven heads with ten horns;

- The beast described as "*was, and is not; and is about to come up out of the abyss*" (Rev. 17:8) is himself an eighth king, which is of the seven (Rev. 17:11);

- The identity of the beast with two horns like a lamb is to be searched on the territory where empires prophetically described as *"leopard, bear, and lion"* were once located, as this beast *"exercises all the authority of the first beast in his sight"* (Rev. 13:12); therefore, prophetic characteristics of the first beast are also attributed to the second beast;

- The beast with two horns like a lamb is also described as the *"false prophet"* (Rev. 19:20; 20:10);

- Prophetic allegory *"the woman (harlot) – Babylon the Great"* has a very particular characteristic: *"drunken with the blood of the saints, and with the blood of the martyrs of Jesus"* (Rev. 17:6); *"in her was found the blood of prophets and of saints"* (Rev. 18:24);

- The *"woman (great city)"* sits on seven mountains, not seven hills; the *"seven mountains"* represent seven kings or kingdoms (Rev. 17:9-10);

- The *"woman (harlot)"* sits on many *"waters"*; these waters represent *"peoples, and multitudes, and nations, and tongues"* (Rev. 17:1, 15);

- The ten horns and the beast will hate the harlot (great city), destroy her, and burn her with fire (Rev. 17:16; Rev. 18:20-21);

Most of the prophecies of Revelation have already been fulfilled; however, certain prophetic events must yet occur before the return of our Lord Jesus Christ. Until then, controversy and speculative arguments regarding the fulfillment of Bible prophecy must continue. However, those believers who analyze prophetic messages *"in spirit and in truth"*, let them understand the prophecy and be holy.

> *"16 because it is written, [i]Ye shall be holy; for I am holy" (1Pet. 1:16; Lev. 11:44-45; 19:2; 20:7).*

Bibliography

The Holy Bible, American Standard Version (ASV)

The Holy Bible, World English Bible (WEB)

[1] "Seven hills of Rome." *Wikipedia: The Free Encyclopedia*. Wikimedia Foundation, Inc. 15 June 2016. 2016. Web. 4 July 2016. <http://en. wikipedia.org.wiki/Seven_hills_of_Rome>

[2] "Seven hills of Istanbul." *Wikipedia: The Free Encyclopedia*. Wikimedia Foundation, Inc. 16 April 2016. Web. 4 July 2016. <http://en. wikipedia.org.wiki/Seven_hills_of_Istanbul>

[3] Seven heads and ten horns - Jesus Messiah. Web. 4 July 2016. <http://jesus-messiah.com/prophecy/rev-13.html>

[4] "List of cities claimed to be built on seven hills." *Wikipedia: The Free Encyclopedia*. Wikimedia Foundation, Inc. 15 June 2016. Web. 20 April 2016. <http://en.wikipedia.org.wiki/List_of_cities_ claimed_to_be_built_on_seven_hills>

[5] "Kaaba." Wikipedia: *The Free Encyclopedia*. Wikimedia Foundation, Inc. 24 June 2016. Web. 4 July 2016. <http:// en.wikipedia.org/ wiki/Kaaba>

[6] "Qibla." *Wikipedia: The Free Encyclopedia*. Wikimedia Foundation, Inc. 31 May 2016. Web. 4 July 2016. <http: // en.wikipedia.org/ wiki/Qibla>

[7] "United States Declaration of independence." *Wikipedia: The Free Encyclopedia*. Wikimedia Foundation, Inc. 12 June 2016. Web. 4 July 2016. <http://en.wikipedia.org/wiki/United_ States_Declaration_ of_Independence

[8] "Islamic calendar." *Wikipedia: The Free Encyclopedia*. Wikimedia Foundation, Inc. 5 July 2016. Web. 6 July 2016. <http://en. wikipedia. org/wiki/Islamic_calendar>